The Un-Saved Christian

The Cost of Disobedience

Rebecca Ruth

Edited by Orville Stout

This book is dedicated to my precious husband, Scott,

for his

endless,

unconditional love

and

encouragement,

and to our children,

Matthew, Zachary, Danielle, Benjamin, Scotty, Amy, Jerry, Adam,
Ray Lynn, and Jonathan.

I love you all with my life.

CONTENTS

ACKNOWLEDGMENTS

Many thanks to Orville Stout, Media Production Associates, for editing this work. I thought I did fairly well until you got hold of it!

Thank you to all who opened their hearts and shared their personal stories with me. Your courage is inspiring.

Thank you to my parents who took us kids to church at a very early age and introduced us to the King of Kings and Lord of Lords. Because of you, we all know Jesus today.

Most of all, thank you to my Lord and Savior Jesus Christ for never giving up on me and giving me the opportunity to lead others to His Word.

FROM THE AUTHOR

Who but a sinner could write a book about sin? In these last days when the world adopts more and more sins as the "norm" and labels them "OK" we need God's truth more than ever. The church needs to stop trying to look like the world to get people saved and get back to teaching the gospel of the saving grace of Jesus Christ so Christians will know how to live. The "once saved, always saved" theology is incorrect. It is not in the Bible. In fact, the Bible says the opposite is true. You absolutely can lose your salvation by not following Jesus. His blood and His grace and His mercy are not to be taken for granted. When we continue in our sins after salvation, we are crucifying Him over and over. I am talking about unrepentant lifestyle sins that you live in every day that are contrary to the Word of God. By not telling the whole truth, the church is sweet-talking us straight to hell. They are feeding our itching ears what we want to hear, that is that it is ok to sin because God will always forgive us. The part they leave out is that if we die in our unrepentant sins, we will not be saved even though we are believers.

1

Isaiah 30:15 This is what the sovereign Lord, the Holy One of Israel, says: "In repentance and rest is your salvation, in quietness and trust is your strength, but you would have none of it."

In repentance and rest is your salvation. The whole Bible teaches repentance. That means you change your mind about your sin and make a decision to follow Jesus. You choose to live your life His way instead of yours so you stop doing the things the Bible calls "sin." We live our lives in the Sabbath rest of Jesus every day. We don't have to earn our salvation by fulfilling laws or works because Jesus fulfilled the work of salvation for us. We are not under the law of the Israelites because of the cross.

Galatians 5:16-18 So I say, live by the Spirit, and you will not gratify the desires of the sinful nature. For the sinful nature desires what is contrary to the Spirit and the Spirit what is contrary to the sinful nature. They are in conflict with each other, so that you do not do what you want. But if you are led by the Spirit, you are not under law.

Our behavior after we get saved is repentance and rest. We are led by the Holy Spirit. You only find this out if you read the Bible for yourself and don't rely on the church to speak the whole truth. We need churches to rise up and teach the truth that sin is not ok. If you are Christians living sinfully, the Bible says you are going to hell if you don't repent and you die in that condition.

Matthew 7:21-23 "Not everyone who says to me, 'Lord, Lord,' will enter the kingdom of heaven, but only he who does the will of my Father who is in heaven. Many will say to me on that day, 'Lord, Lord, did we not prophesy in your name and in your name drive out demons and perform many miracles?' Then I will tell them plainly, 'I never knew you. Away from me, you evildoers!'"

Somehow we have come to believe that the only thing we must do to be saved is ask and believe. That's true! But after the "I believe" commitment there is an "evildoer" problem to be dealt

2

with. Think of church leaders whose sin has been exposed here. It is God who exposes sin. The discipline as sons and daughters of God is to give us a chance to get it right with Him. There is a putting away of our old selves that accompanies salvation. The thief on the cross had it easy. He didn't have to consider a lifestyle of repentance and obedience. He got saved and was with Jesus that day. The church is good at getting people saved. It is good at the touchy feely stuff like how much God loves you and how He will take care of you and give you the desires of your heart, but it is all about how much God loves us and what He will do for us and so very little on what we must do to love Him back. When we live for God our lives are so much better. When we give up our sins, there is joy not misery.

Ultimately, your salvation is on your own head. It is not the responsibility of the church, your parents, friends, spouse or anyone else but you. That is the beauty of the Word of God. If you want absolute truth and love, read the second greatest present that God gave to you personally. His love letter to the world so that everyone will know the truth and be set free. It is the Christmas present you never got, the Easter basket you always wanted, the Valentine you never received, the words you always wanted to hear. It is the birthday present your spouse or your family never gave you, the love you have been looking for your whole life. It is the salve for your wounds that won't heal and the truth you couldn't find that has the power to set you free. The first greatest present that God gave you is His Son, Jesus. He is the ribbon that holds all of God's gifts together. But you can't just read it, you must obey it. Jesus is your salvation and the Bible is His love letter to you and your life instruction manual. Then you can tell others the good news, too. That is that Jesus loves you and died for all your sins so you can be saved and live in eternity with Him forever.

I am a sinner saved by grace. I have learned that I cannot go on sinning if I want to go to heaven. I have to change my way to His way. The things that come out of my mouth must be followed by my actions. My actions and the things that come out of my mouth must follow the Word of God that I have stored in my heart. To go to heaven, I must obey God. I have to learn to master sin so it doesn't master me, and I must walk in love. If I am truly saved, I will walk in love because His Holy Spirit is in me and the fruit of the Holy Spirit will show in my life. When I blow it, I have to repent and ask Jesus to forgive me so I can move on in Him.

1 Corinthians 13:1-13 If I speak in the tongues of men or of angels, but do not have love, I am only a resounding gong or a clanging cymbal. If I have the gift of prophecy and can fathom all mysteries and all knowledge, and if I have a faith that can move mountains, but do not have love, I am nothing. If I give all I possess to the poor and give over my body to hardship that I may boast, but do not have love, I gain nothing. Love is patient, love is kind. It does not envy, it does not boast, it is not proud. It does not dishonor others, it is not self-seeking, it is not easily angered, it keeps no record of wrongs. Love does not delight in evil but rejoices with the truth. It always protects, always trusts, always hopes, always perseveres. Love never fails. But where there are prophecies, they will cease; where there are tongues, they will be stilled; where there is knowledge, it will pass away. For we know in part and we prophesy in part, but when completeness comes, what is in part disappears. When I was a child, I talked like a child, I thought like a child, I reasoned like a child. When I became a man, I put the ways of childhood behind me. For now we see only a reflection as in a mirror; then we shall see face to face. Now I know in part; then I shall know fully, even as I am fully known. And now these three remain: faith, hope and love. But the greatest of these is love.

Isn't that beautiful? The greatest love of all is not "loving yourself" like the song says. Nowhere in the Bible does it say to love yourself. We all do way too much of that. It says to love the Lord your God with all your heart, soul, mind and strength. Then we are to love others as much as we love ourselves.

Mark 12:30-31 "Love the Lord your God with all your heart and

4

with all your soul and with all your mind and with all your strength.'
The second is this: 'Love your neighbor as yourself.' There is no
commandment greater than these."

We are to copy God's love for us by passing that same love out to others so they can be saved too. There is a reason for us to love just as there was a reason for God to sacrifice His only Son on the cross for us in love; heaven. We do not love for nothing. Sometimes reaching out in love is telling Christians they are going to hell. It is not popular. Christians don't like being told they are going to hell. That is why preachers steer clear of it. But some Christians hear it and do something about it. So I am taking a deep breath and writing this book in love to tell you that if you don't walk with God and obey His Word, you are a "Christian" who is going to hell.

I wrote this book because I was amazed at how many children who were raised in the church grew up to live in the world. I was amazed at the lifestyles of people who call themselves "Christians." I wanted to know what happened so I started asking them. I asked one "Christian" girl what she was thinking of when she put battery acid (meth) in her mouth for the first time.

She said, "Nothing!"

So I asked again, "Didn't you feel a check in your spirit or wonder what God would think?"

She said "Nope, I just wanted to party."

So I asked others. "What made you think it is ok to live together instead of getting married?" The answers:

"Because the world is comfortable with it. It is ok now."

"We are saved by grace."

"This is what I have chosen for my life and I just don't believe Jesus would do that to me."

When I ask about getting drunk or doing drugs, there is no fear of God or hell. There was no evidence of the Holy Spirit or a relationship with Jesus in any of them. None of them read their bibles and the other thing they have in common is that they don't go to church anymore. Yet many felt that because they believed Jesus is the Son of God and died for them, they were still saved because of grace. They were right about one thing. Jesus doesn't want them to go to hell. But what they didn't get was that they could send their own selves to hell because they didn't do what Jesus told them to do. Jesus won't recognize them when He comes back. We have getting saved right, but what happens after we get saved is where we get in trouble. The Bible says we are to judge those inside the church not outside. We don't judge non-Christians because we used to be non-Christians ourselves. But we judge inside the church because we have to be careful of the yeast that spreads. The yeast cannot be allowed to remain in our churches so that truth will prevail.

We are in the last days, and the church is not ready. Our churches are filled with couples that are living together unmarried, members who get drunk and do drugs and are filled with immorality. We have members whose mouths speak profanity and think nothing of using God's name in vain. We have churches that are filled with idol worship and lies. Our members are in church on Sundays and in stripper bars on Friday and Saturday. Some churches decorate their yards for Halloween and invite Santa for Christmas. We look like hypocrites to the world, and we are. The one underlying reason is a suffering relationship with Jesus because we do not read our Bibles. We must clean up our churches by teaching the truth of the Word and renewing our relationship with Jesus. The world is getting worse just as the Bible said it would, but a praying army changes things. Let's build an army of prayers who love God and are willing to obey His Word so we can minister to a hurting world in these last days.

If I can help to lead people to the Bible, if I can get people to take an interest in reading the Word of God for themselves, then I have succeeded in my efforts. Even if I am found to be wrong on some counts and someone got saved because they bothered to read not my book, but God's, I rejoice. Salvation for the army of God so we can be a powerhouse of prayer in these last days is the absolute goal of this book. It is to lead you to the Bible, which has salvation as its goal. If after starting this, you decide you don't want to finish it, good! Toss my book aside and go straight to God's Word. It will save you a lot of time, and time is exactly what we are short of.

One day I was in a store and there were a bunch of books scattered around on the bottom shelf of a display. They were not neatly standing in a row, but rather they were thrown there. I saw in the heap a book written by a Christian author I greatly respect. I said, "Oh Lord! That book shouldn't be there! Is this where my book will end up?" I was sad at the location of the book, the condition of the shelf and the shelf being so close to the floor. Then I looked down at the shelf again and there lay a Bible. You know how sometimes God shows you something and you get it all at once, instant revelation in a pile? This was that time. Instantly I saw what God saw. It was this: All stores get visited by people that need God, so the location of the books at that store was perfect. The disarray on the shelf created a divine display that allowed the titles to be read without searching through the books, so the condition of the shelf was perfect. The bottom shelf level was just right for eyes of any height to fall on, so the bottom shelf was perfect. Both books were at the right place, in the right place, at the right height, displayed in the right way so that the condition of the world might be divinely changed. And finally, if God could put His book there, He could put mine there, too. Hallelujah! Now I pray that this book will be divinely displayed anywhere and that the reader will get so excited about reading the Word of God, they won't even finish this one!

INTRODUCTION

This book assumes that you call yourself a "Christian." It is written for you. It is for Christian believers and deals with life after salvation. What did you do with your new salvation choice? It is a call for Christians everywhere to re-read our Bibles and get serious about our faith so we can be a powerful, praying army for God in these last days. It is a call to put aside the world and draw closer to God as we build a relationship with His son Jesus. That can only be done by burying ourselves in His Word so we will know how God wants us to live. If we don't read our Bibles, we can't build our faith as we get to know the One who saved us. If we continue as we are, some of us are going to be very surprised on the day of the Lord's return.

Jesus is coming soon and His reward is with Him. He is going to give to you according to what you have done with your salvation. What are your deeds now that you are saved? How did your life change? Did you wash your robes so that you would have the right to go into heaven? You have no right to go through the gates into the city of heaven with dirty robes. You will be left outside and counted among the unbelievers. Jesus sent his angel to give this testimony to the churches, not the unbelievers. It will be too late for them. This warning is for the ones in robes (Revelation 22:14-15).

When you got saved you were clothed with garments of salvation and arrayed in a robe of righteousness (Isaiah 61:10). Because He loves us, God made a way for us to come to Him through Jesus Christ and the blood He shed on the cross. You have been saved by grace (Gods kindness) through your faith. It was a gift. You didn't earn it by works. You cannot think to yourself, "I am a good person. Surely God will accept me because of the things I have done and not done." You got saved because you said you believed that Jesus is the Son of God and you believed that His shed blood saved you from all your sins. The righteous live by faith and without faith it is impossible to please Him (Hebrews 11:6). It is a heart condition, a love relationship between you and the Father. You confessed your sins and you were made a new creation. You were dead in your sins, but now you are alive in Christ. You belong to Him. But there is a problem. You didn't put off your old self.

Ephesians 4:22-24 You were taught in regard to your former way of life to put off your old self which is being corrupted by its deceitful desires; to be made new in the attitude of your minds; and to put on the new self, created to be like God in true righteousness and holiness.

Instead of doing what pleases God, you continued to please yourself. You ignored His Word and are still doing your own thing. You are supposed to put off your old self and have a new attitude in your mind. You think that because you got saved you are now free to do anything you want because the blood covers you and, therefore, God is obligated to save you. The Bible calls you an enemy of God. You need to know something:

Hebrews 10:26-31 If we deliberately keep on sinning after we have received the knowledge of the truth, no sacrifice for sins is left, but only a fearful expectation of judgment and of raging fire that will consume the

10

enemies of God. Anyone who rejected the Law of Moses died without mercy on the testimony of two or three witnesses. How much more severely do you think a man deserves to be punished who has trampled the Son of God under foot, who has treated as an unholy thing the blood of the covenant that sanctified him, and who has insulted the Spirit of grace? For we know Him who said, "It is mine to avenge; I will repay," and again, "The Lord will judge his people." It is a dreadful thing to fall into the hands of the living God.

Our God is a consuming fire. We are to worship Him with reverence and awe. We are to work out our salvation with fear and trembling. If we shrink back, we will be destroyed.

Hebrews 10:38-39 But my righteous one will live by faith. And if he shrinks back, I will not be pleased with him. But we are not of those who shrink back and are destroyed, but of those who believe and are saved.

1 John 4:9 This is how God showed His love among us: He sent His one and only Son into the world that we might live through Him.

Why did you get saved and you are still doing evil? Why are you still obeying the lusts of the flesh after you learned the truth? Why is the world still attractive to you? It is not those who hear the law who are righteous in God's sight, but it is those who obey the law who will be declared righteous (Romans 2:13). "Righteous" means to be right with God. To be saved, you must be right with God. That means we do not let sin rule us because we are controlled by the Holy Spirit. Our minds are set on the things the Spirit desires. Those controlled by the sinful nature cannot please God (Romans 8:8). If you live according to the sinful nature, you will die (Romans 8:1-17). The enemy didn't snatch your salvation from you. You willingly gave it up. That is what this book is all about.

Jeremiah 7:23 Obey me, and I will be your God and you will be my people. Walk in all the ways I command you that it may go well with you.

God tells us that if we will just walk in *His* way, it will go well with us. He knows what will happen to us if we don't, and He loves us too much to let that happen, so He disciplines us as His sons and daughters (Hebrews 12:1-17).

In the end, when it's all said and done, if you want God to recognize you, you have to look like His Son. Your attitude should be the same as that of Christ Jesus. You cannot be in the presence of Jesus and not be changed. You will begin to be convicted of your sins and they won't feel right anymore. Your soul will be stirred to change things. Instead of sowing to please your sinful nature, which reaps destruction, you will sow to please the Spirit and reap eternal life.

Love for God means to obey His commands. If you are truly born again, you will not continue in sin. The love of Jesus will break your heart and you will live to please Him not your old sinful nature. The things you do will change because you are now doing things that please God. It feels better inside when you live to please God. You begin to see the fruit of your salvation. Things that didn't make sense before begin to gel because you are forming a relationship with the Father. God knows your name! It is written in His book.

If your actions don't change, your faith is dead and your salvation was just a formality – something you did for a moment with a wagging tongue and half a heart but no real conviction. Your life didn't change. You are still living to please your sinful nature. You wonder why God doesn't change things for you. God is waiting for you to put away the old self and follow Him. God doesn't owe you anything. He has already put it all out there and all we have to do is lay hold of it. You expect miracles and blessings and for God to be your servant and for everything to just fall into place, but God does not recognize you. You are not living by the Spirit, and so you are gratifying the desires of the sinful nature.

Galatians 5:19-21 The acts of the sinful nature are obvious: sexual immorality, impurity and debauchery; idolatry and witchcraft; hatred, discord, jealousy, fits of rage, selfish ambition, dissensions, factions and envy; drunkenness, orgies, and the like. I warn you, as I did before, that those who live like this will not inherit the kingdom of God.

Galatians 5:24-25 Those who belong to Christ Jesus have crucified the sinful nature with its passions and desires. Since we live by the Spirit, let us keep in step with the Spirit.

Paul is warning Christians about their behavior after they are saved. If you belong to Christ Jesus you will crucify the sinful nature. You will choose God's way instead of your own. You cannot live like the world and go to heaven. If you were sincere, you received the Spirit of God. He gave that to you so you would understand things the world cannot comprehend. The world wants God to live up to their expectations. But God is our Creator and knows all things. He absolutely loves to blow us away with His wisdom. As Christians, God shares His wisdom with us through His Holy Spirit so we can know the secret things.

1Corinthians 2:6-16 We do however, speak a message of wisdom among the mature, but not the wisdom of this age or of the rulers of this age, who are coming to nothing. No, we speak of God's secret wisdom, a wisdom that has been hidden and that God destined for our glory before time began. None of the rulers of this age understood it, for if they had, they would not have crucified the Lord of glory. However, as it is written: "No eye has seen, no ear has heard, no mind has conceived what God has prepared for those who love Him" (Isaiah 64:4). But God revealed it to us by his Spirit. The Spirit searches all things, even the deep things of God. For who among men knows the thoughts of a man except the man's spirit within him? In the same way no one knows the thoughts of God except the Spirit of God. We have not received the spirit of the world but the Spirit who is from God, that we may understand what God has freely given us. This is what we speak, not in words taught us by human wisdom but in words taught by the spirit, expressing spiritual truths in spiritual words. The man without the Spirit does not accept the things that come from the Spirit of God, for they are foolishness to him, and he cannot understand them, because they are spiritually discerned. The spiritual man makes judgments about all things, but he himself is not subject to any man's judgment: "For who has known the mind of the Lord that he may instruct him?" But we have the mind of Christ.

When you got saved, you received the mind of Christ. You may not have felt anything earth shattering but you got it. Your job now is to learn to recognize His voice. When you get a new friend you learn to recognize your friend's voice by spending time together. Jesus is your new friend. You learn to recognize His voice by reading the Bible. As you get to know Him, you will be able to spiritually discern things you did not understand before. You have the wisdom, and the thoughts and the mind of Christ. Your body is now God's temple and God's Spirit lives in you.

God does wonderful, marvelous things for His people. Gideon defeated the Midianites and the Amalekites with three hundred men, some trumpets, torches, and jars. The walls of Jericho fell with the shouts of the people. The waters parted for the Israelites. They drank water from a rock. The ark on dry land saved Noah and his family from the flood. The widow's oil pots were supernaturally filled. The Shunammite's son was raised from the dead. Shadrach, Meshach and Abednego didn't burn in the fire. Daniel was safe in the lion's den. Jesus healed people and cast demons out of them and taught His disciples to do the same. He turned water into wine. Then, the most amazing miracle of all, He died and rose again for us. Oh, when you find out what that really means, your life will be changed forever. God loves surprising us with His miracles. He never stopped doing miracles. He still saves, heals and delivers. He is the same yesterday, today and forever. Do not listen to the world. They don't know the things of God. God can't wait to do miracles in your life. Read your Bible and learn about God. Make another decision to follow Christ, only make it real this time and don't shrink back (Hebrews 10:35-39).

Dear Heavenly Father, I have sinned against you. I did not walk in your ways and I did not obey your Word. I followed my own way, the ways of the world and I broke your heart. I treated the cross of Jesus like it was nothing and followed the selfishness of my heart to get my own way even though I knew deep inside it was wrong. Lord God I want you in my life. I am so sorry for my sins. Please forgive me for_____. I renounce my old way of life and I choose to follow you. Make my life a testimony to you Lord so others will see you in me. Fill me with your precious Holy Spirit and give me faith so I can rightly discern your Word. Please teach me all your ways and fill me with your love and compassion so I can lead others to Christ. Thank you for forgiving me. Thank you, Jesus, for dying on the cross for me. Thank you for your Holy Spirit. Thank you for coming into my heart and giving me a new life. Amen.

PROLOGUE
THE FENCE LINE

There is a fence line between good and evil. It is but a hairs width. On one side is destruction and on the other victory. It is a bittersweet victory because no one should get to the fence in the first place, especially a Christian.

The fence represents the final step in your decision to do what's right or to choose evil. If you get to the fence, it is almost too late already. You got to the fence by entertaining temptation and it has gone so far, all that is left is a yes or a no. It is where you end up when you have completed all of your wrong thinking. The final warning siren before your fate is sealed, one last decision to make before life or death, heaven or hell. You do not fall off the fence. Any decision that is made there is a deliberate choice. You jump to one side or the other. It is no accident.

Compromise, self-indulgence, and selfishness got you to the fence. Instead of running for your life, you entertained just one more thought. Your spirit knows the truth, but your flesh is bigger and knows what's better and only one of them can win.

17

Besides, it feels so good. Getting to the fence is three-quarters failure and one-quarter last chance – shame on you.

There never should have been a battle. Your very first compromising thought should have been thrown out immediately – not even finished. You went too far. The thought makes sense now. It is not so bad. No one will know. It is nobody's business. Everybody does it. My parents don't seem to mind. It's normal, times change. God will forgive me, cheap grace.

At the fence line things are different. A final decision is made. There will be no more deciding. No more thinking about it. This is it, your choice. Whatever you choose, it will change your life forever and usually the lives of those around you.

You think differently after you have encountered the fence. No matter which side you choose, there is always the realization of "what if." What if I had not made this choice? What if I made the other choice? Both are related to horror. The fence line between right and wrong is so minuscule, so tiny, so life changing, it takes your breath away to reflect on it. The wrong choice is wrought with despair and grief and regret, the anguish of it almost unbearable. The right choice brings peace, relief and blessings. But oddly enough, it leaves a scar that serves as a constant reminder of the trip to the fence and the choice that was almost made there. The right choice is bitter sweet because it was so close. You will never forget the sin that got you to the fence. Your heart will always break for those who choose the other side. The other side could have been you. You will never point a finger again because you were there. You are no better than the one who chose differently. But you are better off.

Once upon a time I was lying in the sun with my eyes closed and the Lord showed me a vision. There were very bright flames of orange and yellow jumping up and down. At first I thought it was just the brightness of the sun playing tricks on my eyelids. But then I saw figures like paper dolls moving sideways, left to right, head to foot, and head to foot in a constant line through the flames.

18

I said, "That's pretty Lord. What is it?"
He said, "Souls of men."
I said, "What are they doing?"
He said, "They are being glorified."
I said, "Oh. What are they doing now?" because the figures had
gone away but the flames remained.
He said, "You have not gone through the fire yet."
I said, "Will I be glorified when I do?"
He said, "That is up to you."
I said, "I choose to be glorified" and I wept.

I was on the fence. The shame of it has never left me. The scar
that is and could have been burns still. Even though I chose
rightly no numbers of years will erase the horror of how close I
came. I am no better than the one who chose differently but I am
better off. I am healed and forgiven. I have love, joy, peace,
patience, and all the fruits of the Holy Spirit. I have blessings
without number.

The fence is not bigger than God. You can jump to the wrong
side and all is not lost. It just hurts more. It is a stone's throw to
eternal hell there. So many people get hurt. It takes so long to get
home. It is so much harder. What if you die on the wrong side of
the fence?

Come away from the fence. If the fence is in the distance, turn
around. Run home fast! Don't look back. If you jumped to the
wrong side, jump back over! Home is wonderful.

It is the intent of this book to encourage Christians to actually
be Christians so God can use you in His army in these last days. It
is to try and get you to read your Bible every day so that you will
know the truth and your relationship with God will grow and
cultivate a testimony that will win others to Christ. Its purpose is
to bring you back to the foot of the cross in repentance and
holiness, to see again the face of Jesus and return you to your first
love.

Come home, before it's too late.

Chapter 1
The Army of God – Mastering Sin

Isaiah 66:2b
"This is the one I esteem: he who is humble and contrite in spirit,
and trembles at my word."

Thy kingdom come, thy will be done on earth as it is in heaven (Matthew 6:10). Thy kingdom come: the place where God resides. Thy will be done: His will, not ours. On earth as it is in heaven: the same things that God has going on in heaven are to be going on here on earth, too. It is the very great joy of the saints, the redeemed, the sanctified, set apart made holy ones, to carry out the will of the Father here on earth as it is in heaven.

To know the will of the Father we have to read His Word. His instructions are in it. It is living and active. Through His Word, we live and breathe and have our being. The Word of God is the sword of the Spirit, one of our weapons in warfare. It has divine power to demolish strongholds. By His Word the army of

God is to rise up and be forceful men and women who take the kingdom by force (Matthew 11:12). Do you tremble at His Word?

Where is the army of God? Army; one united front, one people who will honor his name and His Word and stand in front of sin and declare, "Who is this uncircumcised Philistine who dares to defy the army of the living God? " Where is the precious remnant that has not bowed their knees to Baal? One God, one Jesus, one Holy Spirit, one Word, one plan, one glorious unified army, called the "church." Is God's army just a remnant?

Matthew 24:35 Heaven and earth will pass away but my words will never pass away.

Indeed they have not. The Word of God is as relevant today as ever. To find out where the church has gone wrong we have to read the Bible. We don't have to go far. God didn't hide it from us. He gave us the key to spiritual success and life happiness right there at the very beginning of the book. Two scriptures to build His army on that would enable that army to take the kingdom by force.

Adam and Eve had one law. Nothing could have been simpler.

Genesis 2:17 But you must not eat of the tree of the knowledge of good and evil for when you eat of it you will surely die.

Adam and Eve thought it was a physical death. Enter the snake. He set things straight for them. Or so they thought.

Genesis 3:4-5 "You will not surely die," the serpent said to the woman. "For God knows that when you eat of it your eyes will be opened, and you will be like God, knowing good and evil."

There is nothing wrong with temptation as long as you don't entertain it. Adam and Eve knew the fruit was there all along, but it took the subtle push of the enemy to ultimately make them jump. They probably never really paid attention to it. Now the fruit is not only good for food, but you can even be like God! Adam was there the whole time listening. They were on the fence line. They should have called God. "Hey God, we have a question." God knew what was going on. He was watching. True love is freedom of choice. They didn't have to ask God anything. They already knew the answer was no. All they had to do was turn around and walk away. But they didn't. They jumped over the fence and ate the fruit. What a disaster!

So Adam and Eve are kicked out of the wonderful Garden of Eden, they have to work hard for their food, and they have children. They are painfully aware of sin and separated from God. Their first son is Cain. We know he had an attitude problem, and the birth of his baby brother, Abel, didn't help. God looked with favor on Abel's offering but not on Cain's. Did God love Cain? Very much – so much that God even spoke to Cain and told him the secret of secrets. God gave Cain the answer to the question that mankind would be asking for the rest of time and Cain missed it! To this day, generations have missed it because they do not have a relationship with their Creator. The question is this, "What is the meaning of life and why are we here?"

Genesis 4:6-7 Then the Lord said to Cain, "Why are you angry: Why is your face downcast? If you do what is right, will you not be accepted? But if you do not do what is right, sin is crouching at your door; it desires to have you, but you must master it.

Let's break it down a word or a phrase at a time so we can understand this remarkable conversation with Cain.

<u>Then:</u> After God did not accept Cain's offering, God did not just leave Cain to wonder why. He gave him a second chance, another opportunity for a correct offering. What an awesome God we serve. How many chances did He give Israel? How many chances does He give us?

<u>The Lord:</u> The creator of heaven and earth! God Himself!

Said: Actually spoke.

To Cain: God loved Cain so much that He actually spoke to him. It was to Cain personally. A message that could save Cain from the disaster that would soon come.

Why are you angry: God already knew. Cain knew, too. He was saying to Cain, "Stop and look at the issue." Why are you mad? Say it out loud. What did *you* do to get yourself in this frame of mind?

Why is your face downcast: Where is your joy? Why are things in your life not going well? What is it that is upsetting you? Go to the root of the problem.

If: This would be conditional.

You: This is about me only. It is not about not the person I was with or the person next to me or anybody else. It is about me personally and the choices I willfully choose to make.

Do what is right: Ask yourself, "Was what I did right or wrong? How do I do this right? What does God say is right? What is an acceptable offering to the Lord?"

Will you not be accepted: If I had done what was right, God would have accepted my offering. I would have been accepted in heaven, and on earth, by my God, by my church, by my family, by my friends, by my co-workers, and by myself. I would not feel bad inside and my face would not be downcast. I would be ready for whatever comes next.

But: There is another option. You have a choice to make. The choice is yours because true love, God's love, is freedom of choice. You can freely choose to do His will instead of your own. He will not force Himself on you.

If: It's conditional again.

You do not do what is right: If you choose wrong even though you know better. If you make a conscious, deliberate decision to do what God has said not to do. The Bible calls it presumptuous sin.

Sin: What God has said you cannot do.

24

Is crouching at your door: The word "crouching" means to get down low to the ground in a position ready to spring. Picture a demon hiding behind a closed door ready to jump on you when you come through. Sin is always there and ready for you. It is not an inanimate object, but it is a living thing crouching at your door. It crouches because if it were to stand up straight in plain sight you would recognize it as sin and turn around and run. So it has to hide behind a closed door. It tries to disguise itself. All you have to do is say yes and open the door for sin to spring into action, simple. In the garden the temptation was not the sin. The sin came out of what they did with the temptation. Sin is an action. It is obedience to temptation. Satan is called the Tempter. He cannot force you to sin. He can only tempt you. It is interesting that to "crouch" also means to get in a position of humility or fear. Satan and his demons are terrified that you will choose correctly.

It desires: Sin wants, it would like, it craves, wishes, yearns for, covets, but notice it doesn't say it "will" have you. That is because it needs your permission. Freedom of choice, remember? But don't confuse free choice with free will. You do not have free will. You choose to give up your will for the will of Jesus when you use your freedom of choice to follow Him.

To have you: Possess you, own you, and control you for as long as you will allow. Sin has a personality. It is pure evil. It wants you as far away from heaven as it can get you. The longer you entertain temptation, the stronger it gets. Temptation is very powerful. The whole goal, the total drive of Satan, every fiber of his being is focused on keeping souls out of heaven. He is very aware of his future and he is very aware of yours. He knows he was defeated at the cross and he is furious to this day. He will do anything in his power to keep you from the promises of God. If Satan can get you to say yes to sin, he owns you for as long as you will allow him to.

But: Now it is getting exciting! This is a huge word! There is a "but!" God has given us a way out. There is a condition, a loophole, another way, a key, a safety net. What is it?

You: The answer lies with me. Nobody else is mentioned. It is totally up to me.

Must: There is no choice. There is no other way. I have to do this whether I like it or not or I will die.

Master: Have absolute control over, have power over, have absolute authority over, rule over, lord over, govern, be the boss of, dictate, be excellent about, be highly skilled in, know everything about, be able to defeat, able to break the will of. I am the boss of my temptations. I must have a PhD in controlling sin. Sin does not control me. The answer to any sin is a quick and decisive no! I have to recognize sin so clearly, that it becomes second nature. I have to recognize it no matter what it is disguised in. Not only do I have to recognize it, I have to learn to deal with it so quickly that it is no longer a problem for me. I do not entertain even the smallest of temptations so it does not become sin. I must know everything there is to know about conquering sin. I am to be a master temptation thrower-outer! The Bible tells me everything I need to know about recognizing and mastering "it."

It: Sin. Period. All sins, every temptation known to mankind. Everything that God said we cannot do.

Notice God does not give a name to Cain's sin. That is because it includes all sins, every act that goes against the law of God. All sin leads to death. Sin is alive. It is a living act of disobedience. Sin enters disguised as an innocent temptation, just a little thought. But God tells us through Cain that we must master it. It is not enough to be mildly aware of sin and temptation. I must master it. If I don't, I will fall when I am tempted. The Bible has so much to say about our thoughts.

We cannot master sin by ourselves so God gave us the perfect weapons.

Revelation 12:11 "They overcame him (Satan) by the blood of the Lamb and by the word of their testimony."

Your weapons in warfare are the blood of Jesus, name of Jesus, the Word of God, and the power of your testimony. That is how you fight temptation.

2 Corinthians 10:3-5 For though we walk in the flesh, we do not war after the flesh: For the weapons of our warfare are not carnal, but mighty through God to the pulling down of strongholds; casting down imaginations, and every high thing that exalteth itself against the knowledge of God, and bringing into captivity every thought to the obedience of Christ.

Cain's thoughts were stuck on how God accepted his little brother's offering and not his. Instead of bringing every thought into captivity, Cain wallowed in them and nursed them until they grew into ridiculous proportions and actually made sense to him. His thoughts became a stronghold that needed to be pulled down and taken captive to the obedience of Christ.

Satan loves nothing more than destroying the testimony of the saints. But Jesus died for your testimony. His one blood sacrifice conquered the enemy forever and covered all your sins. He shed His precious blood so that your testimony would have a happy ending. What did Cain and his family have? They had God Himself to help them master sin.

Instead of listening to God and taking the second chance for acceptance, Cain kills Abel. Jealousy, anger, bitterness, selfishness and temptation drove him to the fence line and he dove over. Notice these feelings only take him to the fence line. He had to make the decision once he got there to dive over. And dive he did!

In verses six and seven God spoke to Cain and told him he must master sin. In the very next verse, verse eight, Cain says to Abel, "Let's go out to the field." What in the world? Didn't Cain say anything to God? Was there no discussion? How is it that

Cain would have a discussion with temptation and not God? How much time was there between verses seven and eight? This is terrifying. Cain left the presence of his holy God who spoke to him and told him the secret of secrets and went and murdered his brother. We don't know how much time there was between his visit with God and the murder, but every second you spend on the fence line is one more opportunity to turn around and run for your life, literally. Or, it is one step closer to death. Cain had to find Abel. How much time did that take? What was he thinking on the way? Then, they had to go to the field. How far away was that? Now they are walking together. What did they talk about? Where is the compassion? Every footstep, every second is an opportunity to rethink what you are about to do.

Sin acts very quickly. It doesn't require a lot of temptation time to hurl you into the abyss. You have just seconds to judge the thought and throw it out. You are not ignorant of right and wrong. Every thought after the first one becomes stronger and stronger and takes you closer to the fence line. The bible tells us to cast down those thoughts and bring them into the obedience of Christ.

2 Corinthians 10:5 Casting down imaginations, and every high thing that exalteth itself against the knowledge of God, and bringing into captivity every thought to the obedience of Christ.

Ephesians 4:26-27 "In your anger do not sin." Do not let the sun go down while you are still angry, and do not give the devil a foothold.

That verse tells us that if we go to bed at night and we are still mad at something, we are giving the devil a foothold. This is a time issue. Remember sin is alive. Each thought becomes a stronghold. That means that sin is getting a strong hold on you. The longer you entertain the temptation, the stronger the stronghold gets. God said to master sin because you can. Throw out the very first thought. How? Say "no" and think about something else. Don't give it any more of your time. Find a scripture and use it against the thought. You fight the enemy with the Word. We know that is true because Hebrews 4:12 tell us it is.

Hebrews 4:12 For the word of God is living and active. Sharper than any double-edged sword, it penetrates even to dividing soul and spirit, joints and marrow; it judges the thoughts and attitudes of the heart.

To master sin you must know what God's Word says. Satan does. He tried to use the Word against Jesus in Matthew 4, but Jesus knows the Word, too. Jesus is a master temptation thrower-outer! He used the scriptures right back at the devil and won. You do that, too. There was no conversation with the devil. Jesus didn't have to think about Satan's offers and contemplate the outcome. With each temptation Jesus used just one scripture to end the matter. After only three scriptures Jesus defeated Satan.

Matthew 4:10 "Get thee hence Satan: for it is written, Thou shalt worship the Lord thy God, and Him only shalt thou serve."

The third scripture came with an order, "You are dismissed Satan!"

James 4:7 Submit yourselves, then, to God. Resist the devil, and he will flee from you.

You can scare the devil away with the Word of God! Notice also that Satan was tempting Jesus when Jesus had not eaten for forty days and forty nights. Temptation will come when you are weak physically, mentally or spiritually.

Luke 4:13 When the devil had finished all this tempting, he left Him until an opportune time.

The enemy will look for a good time to mess you up. You don't have to be afraid. You just have to be ready. In Matthew 16:23 Jesus was telling His disciples that He would suffer and die and after three days would be raised up again. Peter was horrified and told Jesus that it would never happen. But Jesus immediately cut Peter off. He ended the conversation that could have become a temptation to get out of the cross by commanding Satan to get behind Him.

Matthew 16:23 Jesus turned and said to Peter, "Get behind me, Satan! You are a stumbling block to me; you do not have in mind the things of God, but the things of men."

Peter had no idea how important the blood of Jesus would be. He didn't know that God had a plan from the very beginning of the world that would defeat Satan forever, but Jesus did. Sometimes your temptation will come from your friends or family or people you trust because they have in mind the things of men and not the things of God. If you are not of the Spirit, you cannot understand the ways of the Spirit. Aren't you glad we have the Word? It tells us what the things of God are.

James 1:13-15 When tempted, no one should say, "God is tempting me." For God cannot be tempted by evil, nor does he tempt anyone; but each one is tempted when, by his own evil desire, he is dragged away and enticed. Then, after desire has conceived, it gives birth to sin; and sin, when it is full-grown, gives birth to death.

Here is the good news. It takes no energy at all to hurl the sword of the spirit at sin and win. You can do that laying down or hanging upside down from a tree! But if you don't know what the Bible says, you have no sword. You are powerless against the enemy.

So what was Cain thinking? At the fence line you only think about one thing. You are entertaining the temptation that got you there. To entertain temptation means to play with the idea to see if you can make it work for you somehow. How can I get my own way? The consequences are a very small issue to you at the fence line.

By this time Cain's temptation is so strong he is not hearing God. Are you getting this? What did God tell Cain? He said sin is crouching at your door and it desires to have you, but you must master it. Sin was so close. It was just behind the thought. Cain opened the door by entertaining temptation (the thought) and sin wrapped its ugly talons securely around him and accomplished its will to have him.

In verse ten the Lord said, "What have you done?" It was over. Just like that. The thing had been done. Cain can't take it back. Now what? The horror of it is overwhelming. In just five short verses Cain went from life in the presence of God to spiritual death. In verses eleven and twelve God told Cain he was now under a curse. The thing he loved the most, working the soil, would no longer yield crops for him. He would be a restless wanderer on the earth away from what was left of his family and even worse; he would be separated from the presence of God. Now Cain has something to say. His reply was one of selfishness instead of sorrow.

Genesis 4:13 Cain said to the Lord, "My punishment is more than I can bear. Today you are driving me from the land, and I will be hidden from your presence; I will be a restless wanderer on the earth, and whoever finds me will kill me."

Are you kidding me Cain? God told you if you would do right, you would be accepted, but if you didn't, sin would have you. You chose sin. You've been had! Why are you surprised? You didn't obey God in His presence so why are you worried about being removed from His presence? What would have happened if Cain had said he was sorry and changed his attitude. What if he had repented? He could have. But he didn't and so began the ungodly line of Cain. That one selfish act at the fence line changed the world forever. Fence line decisions never affect just you. Whether you choose right or wrong, everyone around you is affected.

So what is the meaning of life? Why are we here?

Ephesians 2:10 For we are God's handiwork, created in Christ Jesus to do good works, which God prepared in advance for us to do.

We are here to do the will of the Father. You will not be angry or downcast if you do what God says is right. You will be happy in life, blessed, and full of joy. You will be able to get on with the things of God because you are doing the will of the Father, which He prepared in advance for you to do. Then God can accept you in heaven. If you don't do what is right, you will not be accepted and sin will own you and you will perish. The only way to be free of sin is to master it so it does not master you.

The entire rest of the bible hinges on those precious words spoken to Cain all those years ago. All sixty-six books tell us the same thing over and over again. Master sin and live. Bring every thought into the obedience of Christ. Mastering sin is step 1-A to moving on in a relationship with God. It starts with repentance and a turning around from your sins and saying, "OK God. I'm sorry I did that. I'm with you now. I'm not living like that anymore. I choose your way, not mine."

Romans 12:1-2 Therefore, I urge you, brothers, in view of God's mercy, to offer your bodies as living sacrifices, holy and pleasing to God – this is your spiritual act of worship. Do not conform any longer to the pattern of this world, but be transformed by the renewing of your mind. Then you will be able to test and approve what God's will is – his good, pleasing and perfect will.

We are here to worship God. That is the meaning of life. Not only in our hearts and minds with singing and praises, but also in our lifestyle as a spiritual act of worship to Him. Mastering sin is an act of worship. That is how you act justly, love mercy and walk humbly with God.

Micah 6:8 He has showed you, O man, what is good. And what does the Lord require of you? To act justly and to love mercy and to walk humbly with your God.

The army of God that is taking the kingdom by force is here to take as many souls to heaven as we can. We are here to carry out the will of God on earth as it is in heaven. We are to live life abundantly in the fruits of the Holy Spirit (John 10:10). Not just a little to get by but life full of joy, victory, miracles, signs and wonders. We are to master sin so we can spend our lives doing the will of the Father on earth as it is in heaven because life on this earth leads to heaven or hell. How much time do you spend wallowing in the rotting pools of your messes because you have not mastered sin in your life? Are you tired of it yet?

If Adam and Eve could not obey just one rule, how could we obey ten? There is only one way. We must master sin. We can only do that if we have a personal relationship with God through His son Jesus Christ. And that relationship can only be successful if we learn to master sin. They go hand in hand. You learn to master sin by reading your Bible every day. If it were not possible, God would not have told us to do it.

Luke 4:4 And Jesus answered him, saying, it is written, man shall not live by bread alone, but by every word of God.

Deuteronomy 8:3 He humbled you, causing you to hunger and then feeding you with manna, which neither you nor your fathers had known, to teach you that man does not live on bread alone but on every word that comes from the mouth of the Lord.

Jeremiah 15:16 (KJV) Thy words were found, and I did eat them; and thy word was unto me the joy and rejoicing of mine heart: for I am called by thy name, O Lord God of hosts.

Cain did not have the bible to refer to and still he was told he must master sin. Cain had the word God had just given him. He could have used that against the enemy. He could have said, "No, I will not do this thing. I will master sin and do what is right like God just told me. I'm sorry, God for entertaining the thought of murder. Please forgive me and accept my new offering."

When you heard that a great man or woman of God failed in ministry, did you wonder how it was possible? "But they were so used of God! How did that happen?"

You can have a personal relationship with your Heavenly Father and die a spiritual death because you never learned to master sin. Did you get that? It is possible to know God and not have eternal life because you chose sin instead (Ezekiel 18: 21-32).

How long does it take to say no? That is determined by how much time you devote to the temptation. We are not doomed to a life of struggle and hardship because we must spend so much time fighting temptation. Jesus said He came to give us life and life abundantly. That means a full happy life.

Mastering sin does not take a lot of time. You just have to want to do it. Decide first whose side you are on, then practice defeating even the smallest of temptations quickly. When you learn to master sin, you get so good at it that you don't waste time on temptation anymore. Here's the *only* way to a fast and successful "no."

DO NOT HAVE A CONVERSATION WITH TEMPTATION, PERIOD.

You will recognize temptation instantly because you have studied your Bible. The counterfeit will light up like a beacon against the Word of God. There is no discussion. The answer is "no," walk away. Obedience is an action word. This applies whether it is a thought or a person tempting you. It's OK to run away if you must. You don't run in fear, you run in defiance! When you are strong in your faith you can use the "shield of faith wherewith you will quench all the fiery darts of the devil" and the "sword of the spirit which is the Word of God" (Ephesians 6) just like Jesus did. Then turn around, walk away, leave, hang up the phone, turn off the TV or the computer, zero discussion. Do not give the thought any more of your time. As you are walking away praise Him. "Thank you Jesus that you have told me the truth and I did not fall. Thank you Jesus for your Word which is sharper than any double-edged sword. Thank you that it discerns the thoughts and attitudes of the heart. Thank you for the cross." Speak the Word. Pray continually. Share with others what you have learned because that is the power of your testimony in action.

Master sin. If you find you cannot beat it on your own and you need help to overcome it, go tell every righteous pastor, elder, counselor or teacher who will listen about your temptation. Find a stronger Christian than you are to be accountable to. Tell more than one, in the company of more than two, so that if one is in error, another will recognize it. You already know the temptation is wrong. You will recognize wrong council also.

2 Corinthians 11:13-15 For such men are false apostles, deceitful workmen, masquerading as apostles of Christ. And no wonder, for Satan himself masquerades as an angel of light. It is not surprising, then, if his servants masquerade as servants of righteousness. Their end will be what their actions deserve.

If what they say does not line up with the Word of God and allows for compromise because after all, "God loves everyone and will forgive you anyway," run! You are looking for council that says, "You cannot do that because God said no." Godly council will hold you accountable to the Bible. They will pray with you and help you through. They will not compromise with the world.

Mastering sin is fun! Making right choices is wonderful. The hardest part is the second after the thought, right before your choice. They are the same second. The temptation is the first second and the choice is the very next second. It is so fast! Every second between temptation and your choice is your trip to the fence line. It can take two seconds or two weeks. Anything over two seconds is on its way to disaster if you don't stop it.

When you wake up the next day after saying no to temptation and you are safe in your own bed and you think back and know that things could have been much different today, you will be singing the praises of Him who called you out of darkness into His wonderful light (1 Peter 2:9). Praises to God will be rolling off your tongue! There are no messes to clean up. There are no lies to skirt. No apologies to be made. No running or hiding. Nobody is embarrassed, remorseful, pregnant, hurt, offended, ripped off, sick, sad, in jail, in debt, or dead! You can face the day debt free. No baggage, no regrets and no shame.

James 5:13 Is any one of you in trouble? He should pray. Is anyone happy? Let him sing songs of praise.

You can wake up praying for help or you can wake up breathing sighs of relief and singing songs of praise. It is a no-brainer!

The army of God is the strongest when it is on its knees in prayer. There is war in the heavens and there is a big war brewing on earth. You have to decide fast whose side you are on. God is preparing for the biggest battle of all. You call yourself a Christian, but you have not even moved past "should we sleep together." When the unified church learns to master sin, we will no longer be called the remnant. We will be that forceful army that covers the land and takes the kingdom by force. You can be a part of it or not. What God has for us is so much bigger than our everyday issues. Change your issues! He wants us to move past the mundane and get on with the things of God. The things of God are supernatural.

Ephesians 3:10-11 His intent was that now through the church, the manifold wisdom of God, should be made known unto the rulers and authorities in the heavenly realms, according to this eternal purpose which he accomplished in Christ Jesus our Lord.

That verse is astonishing. Even angels and demons don't know what is going to happen next. They have to watch what's going on in the church here on earth to find out the wisdom of God! What is going on in your church? What is going on in your home and your life? Have you learned to master sin? Can God use you? Can He trust you with His Word? Do you want to be strong in the Lord? Our strength is in our faith in God. Faith comes by hearing and hearing by the Word of God. Get past mastering sin so you can move on in the things of God.

Acts 16:5 So the churches were strengthened in the faith and grew daily in numbers.

Romans 4:20-21 Yet he did not waver through unbelief regarding the promise of God, but was strengthened in his faith and gave glory to God, being fully persuaded that God had power to do what he had promised.

Matthew 26:41 "Watch and pray so that you will not fall into temptation. The spirit is willing but the body is weak."

Watchfulness is the price of constant victory. If you want to be victorious, watch.

1 Peter 5:8-9 (KJV) Be sober, be vigilant; because your adversary the devil, as a roaring lion, walketh about, seeking whom he may devour: Whom resist steadfast in the faith, knowing that the same afflictions are accomplished in your brethren that are in the world.

Who does Satan look for to devour? Those that resist steadfast in the faith. Remember Genesis 4:7, "sin desires to have you"? It's the same thing here. The devil seeks whom he may devour. He is looking for Christians who are walking with God who "resist steadfast in the faith." Do you understand that? The devil looks for strong Christians who are obeying God to afflict. Christians who will give him permission to devour them just like he successfully devours people who are in the world. But we are not alone like the people who are in the world. We don't have to be afraid. We have armor on the front and God has our back. We can run into the arms of Jesus when we are tempted and use the Word against the enemy just like Jesus did.

The enemy wants to ruin your testimony. If he can get a Christian into sin, it is another soul that he has won for hell and another testimony ruined. Satan doesn't want Christians to win others to Christ, so he tries to get us to mess up. But the blood of Jesus purchased a way out for us. The blood gives us the opportunity to repent when we fall. It is only too late to repent if you are physically dead. Satan hates the blood of Jesus. He was totally and completely defeated by it. If you are a devoured Christian, repent. Turn around and start over. Don't treat the blood of Jesus as an unholy thing anymore. That blood sanctified you. It set you apart and made you holy for the Master's use.

Hebrews 10:26-29 If we deliberately keep on sinning after we have received the knowledge of the truth, no sacrifice for sins is left, but only a fearful expectation of judgment and of raging fire that will consume the enemies of God. Anyone who rejected the law of Moses died without mercy on the testimony of two or three witnesses. How much more severely do you think a man deserves to be punished who has trampled the Son of God under foot, who has treated as an unholy thing the blood of the covenant that sanctified him, and who has insulted the Spirit of grace?

2 Timothy 1:7 For God did not give us a spirit of timidity, but a spirit of power, of love and of self-discipline.

Satan knows the Word of God but he doesn't "do" the Word of God. Satan can use the scriptures but he won't "do" them. Demons believe so what is to separate you from them if you are not doing what the Bible says?

James 2:19 You believe that there is one God. Good! Even the demons believe that – and shudder.

Only those who do the will of the Father are going to heaven. This is not a "works" salvation. It is a free, grace salvation and a deeds lifestyle. It has to do with your behavior after you get saved. If you truly love God and belong to Him, you will obey Him. When Jesus comes back to get His church, He has to recognize you. You must look like Jesus in the way you live your life. No matter what you are doing now, it is never too late to turn it around. The blood of Jesus cleanses everything. He forgives every sin. Your job is to quit sinning. When you do, you and your household will have peace and joy.

It is never too late to come back to Jesus. Build your testimony. Master sin and truly live.

Chapter 2
The Eyes of the Army of God

Psalm 16:8
I keep my eyes always on the Lord. With Him at my right hand, I will not be shaken.

Psalm 101:3
I will set before my eyes no vile thing.

*D*euteronomy 10:20-22 Fear the Lord your God and serve Him. Hold fast to Him and take your oaths in His name. He is your praise; He is your God, who performed for you those great and awesome wonders you saw with your own eyes. Your forefathers who went down into Egypt were seventy in all, and now the Lord your God has made you as numerous as the stars in the sky.

Deuteronomy 11:1-15 Love the Lord your God and keep His requirements, His decrees, His laws and His commands always. Remember today that your children were not the ones who saw and experienced the discipline of the Lord your God: His majesty, His mighty hand, His outstretched arm; the signs He performed and the things He did in the heart of Egypt, both to Pharaoh king of Egypt and to his whole country; what He did to the Egyptian army, to its horses and chariots, how He overwhelmed them with the waters of the Red Sea as they were pursuing you, and how the Lord brought lasting ruin on them. It was not your children who saw what He did for you in the desert until you arrived at this place, and what He did to Dathan and Abriam, the sons of Eliab the Reubenite, when the earth opened its mouth right in the middle of all Israel and swallowed them up with their households, their tents and every living thing that belonged to them. But it was your own eyes that saw all these great things the Lord has done.

Deuteronomy 11:18-25 Fix these words of mine in your hearts and minds; tie them as symbols on your hands and bind them on your foreheads. Teach them to your children, talking about them when you sit at home and when you walk along the road, when you lie down and when you get up. Write them on the doorframes of your houses and on your gates, so that your days and the days of your children may be many in the land that the Lord swore to give your forefathers, as many as the days that the heavens are above the earth. If you carefully observe all these commands I am giving you to follow – to love the Lord your God, to walk in all His ways and to hold fast to Him – then the Lord will drive out all these nations before you, and you will dispossess nations larger and stronger than you. Every place where you set your foot will be yours: Your territory will extend from the desert to Lebanon and from the Euphrates River to the western sea. No man will be able to stand against you. The Lord your God, as He promised you, will put the terror and fear of you on the whole land, wherever you go.

Joshua 1:8-9 Do not let this Book of the Law depart from your mouth; meditate on it day and night, so that you may be careful to do everything written in it. Then you will be prosperous and successful. Have I not commanded you: Be strong and courageous. Do not be terrified; do not be discouraged, for the Lord your God will be with you wherever you go."

Joshua 2:8-11 Before the spies lay down for the night, she (Rahab) went up on the roof and said to them, "I know that the Lord has given

42

this land to you and that a great fear of you has fallen on us, so that all who live in this country are melting in fear because of you. We have heard how the Lord dried up the water of the Red Sea for you when you came out of Egypt and what you did to Sihon and Og, the two kings of the Amorites east of the Jordan, whom you completely destroyed. When we heard of it, our hearts melted and everyone's courage failed because of you, for the Lord your God is God in heaven above and on the earth below.

Joshua 24:31 Israel served the Lord throughout the lifetime of Joshua and of the elders who outlived him and who had experienced everything the Lord had done for Israel.

Judges 2:10 After that whole generation had been gathered to their fathers, another generation grew up, who knew neither the Lord nor what He had done for Israel.

The only way it was possible for a whole generation to grow up that didn't know the Lord or what He had done for Israel is if the people stopped talking about it and quit reading the book of the law. Even if you didn't see it for yourself and you only heard about, it would feed your faith. Faith lives in your heart. Your eyes and ears fill your mind and your mind sets your faith on fire. The Holy Spirit in your heart testifies to the truth. When we talk about what God has done, we put His picture stories in our minds. What does the battle of Jericho look like to you? How does David and Goliath play out in your mind? You are creating a love relationship between you and God your Father. You are learning to trust Him. What do you set before your eyes and ears to feed your mind that causes your heart to become what it is?

Mark 7:20-23 He went on: "What comes out of a man is what makes him 'unclean.' For from within, out of men's hearts, come evil thoughts, sexual immorality, theft, murder, adultery, greed, malice, deceit, lewdness, envy, slander, arrogance and folly. All these evils come from inside and make a man 'unclean.'"

Not everything in your mind goes to your heart. Algebra is not in my heart. But for people who love math it is because they are emotional about it. An emotion is how you decided to feel about someone or something. You store feelings and emotions in your heart. The things that get into your heart are consuming. When you are in love, it consumes you. When you are angry, it consumes you. When you are scared, it consumes you. When you are worried, it consumes you. When you are hungry or thirsty it consumes you. When you are happy or excited about something it consumes you. These are all feelings that affect the way you behave because they work out their lifecycle in your heart. Generally speaking, the lifecycle of an emotion is short. That is why you have to keep feeding the emotion to keep it alive. (Love, happiness, joy, forgiveness, excitement, motivation, worry, anger, hatred, drugs, alcohol, pornography, sexual immorality, addictions, etc.)

The enemy wants to help you feed your negative emotions so you will make his decisions instead of Gods. It is never too late to change the decisions you have been making because of the emotions you feel. You can change your mind about the decisions you have been making so your emotions fall in line with God's Word.

It is a choice the enemy does not want you to know you have. That is what repentance is. It is changing your mind about sin. You must guard your heart and your mind by being very careful about what you set before your eyes and ears. When something negative happens to you or when wrong opportunity presents itself to you, you must take the feeling or emotion and shelve it for a second so you can make an instant decision about what you are going to do with it. Store it or toss is aside? It's fast! This is where mastering sin comes in. If you deal correctly with it now, you won't have to deal with it later. It will be much bigger later. Remember, yeast grows. For example, if someone says something mean to you, you have the instant choice to hate them or forgive them and move on. If you choose hate, you store hatred in your heart and it stays there until you choose to deal with it. If you choose to forgive, the situation is over. Here is how you know if you have truly forgiven someone: You don't think about it anymore. It doesn't take up any more of your time.

You can store many things in your heart at the same time. The heavier things you store like fear, sadness, anger, bitterness and un-forgiveness and even worldliness, can create a tar pit that compresses the good emotions to the bottom of the heart so it is difficult for them to rise up out of you. No matter how hard you try you cannot pull the good emotions out from under the heaviness of the tar. The tar must be removed first. Our negative emotions must be dealt with at the same time we feel them so they are not allowed to be stored in our hearts as tar. Good and bad emotions cannot exist in the same territory because the tar will influence the good emotions every time unless it is removed. You can choose to get rid of the tar; anger, bitterness and un-forgiveness etc. You can choose to change your mind about the negative feelings. You can pray and ask God to fill you with His wisdom like Solomon did. God loves for us to fill our hearts with His stuff. That is when He can use us. These next three verses are the rise and fall of Solomon. They speak volumes regarding our hearts, eyes, ears and obedience.

1 Kings 10:24 The whole world sought audience with Solomon to hear the wisdom God had put in his heart.

1 Kings 11:2-4 They were from nations about which the Lord had told the Israelites, "You must not intermarry with them, because they will surely turn your hearts after their gods." Nevertheless, Solomon held fast to them in love. He had seven hundred wives of royal birth and three hundred concubines, and his wives led him astray. As Solomon grew old, his wives turned his heart after other gods, and his heart was not fully devoted to the Lord his God, as the heart of David his father had been.

Who you hang out with will influence the decisions you make about God and what you store in your heart. That is why God tells us not to be unequally yoked. This applies to marriage, work, friendships, business, etc. Solomon was hanging out with idolaters and he became one himself. How very sad.

1 Kings 11:9 The Lord became angry with Solomon because his heart had turned away from the Lord, the God of Israel, who had appeared to him twice.

God appeared to Solomon twice! It wasn't that Solomon didn't believe in God. When you have been a Christian for a long time you must not allow yourself to become bored. Solomon had everything. He should have pressed on and kept doing God things but he didn't. He quit storing God things in his heart and feasted his eyes on women; lots of them! He made the choice to worship other gods because he loved his wives more than the living God. That is what he stored in his heart and that is what he and his children became.

Matthew 12:34b For out of the overflow of the heart the mouth speaks.

Your mouth is how you and others know what is in your heart. The things you speak mirror your heart. When your heart is heavy, your shoulders sag, your face is downcast and your arms hang down by your sides. Nothing joyful comes out of your mouth. You are weighed down by the condition of your heart. You have heard of a light heart? That is the heart that is filled with the fruit of the Holy Spirit; love, joy, peace, patience, kindness, goodness, faithfulness, gentleness and self-control. People dance for joy when they are happy. They jump up and down. They sing and the arms go up. Your mind is thinking clearly and is able to deal correctly with the things your eyes and ears are feeding it. Other people can try and feed your heart their emotions but they cannot force you to store them. You have control and it is up to you to guard what you store in your heart. If you store God's Word in your heart, the counterfeit will light up like a beacon. When the enemy tries to plant his junk in your heart you will recognize it and toss it aside.

Matthew 12:35 The good man brings good things out of the good stored up in him and the evil man brings evil things out of the evil stored up in him.

Proverbs 4:20-23 My son pay attention to what I say; listen closely to my words. Do not let them out of your sight. Keep them within your heart; for they are life to those who find them and health to a man's whole body. Above all else, guard your heart, for it is the wellspring of life.

David is telling his son Solomon to not let his words out of his sight. Listen with your ears and write them down and show them to your eyes so you can store them in your heart and remember them because they are life and health to you. More than anything else, the most important thing is to guard your heart because it is the wellspring or fountain of life. What you feed your heart will bubble up out of you and determine your character and the course of your life. You decide what kind of life you live by the things you store in your heart.

Listen to Paul's prayer for the Christians in Ephesus.

Ephesians 3:16-19 I pray that out of his glorious riches he may strengthen you with power through his Spirit in your inner being, <u>so that Christ may dwell in your hearts through faith.</u> And I pray that you, being rooted and established in love, may have power, together with all the saints, to grasp how wide and long and high and deep is the love of Christ, and to know this love that surpasses knowledge—that you may be filled to the measure of all the fullness of God.

Ephesians 1:17-18 I keep asking that the God of our Lord Jesus Christ, the glorious Father, may give you the Spirit of wisdom and revelation, so that you may know Him better. I pray also that <u>the eyes of</u>

your heart may be enlightened in order that you may know the hope to which he has called you, the riches of his glorious inheritance in the saints, and his incomparably great power for us who believe.

If you don't ask Jesus into your heart, you will not be saved. It is by asking Jesus into your heart that the Holy Spirit is able to work in your heart also. Ask the Holy Spirit to fill you up every day so that the eyes of your heart will be enlightened or well informed. Your heart has spiritual eyes that understand truth. When your physical eyes see something, your heart knows the truth about it because the Holy Spirit that lives in your heart gives wisdom and understanding to your mind. Your heart, mind, eyes and ears are all working together to form a rational decision about what you already know. The word "know" is used twice in those verses. That is the renewed mind of a Christian. When a Christian knowingly sins, they have ignored what they know in the heart and mind and followed their eyes and ears. The eyes and ears are the entrance or portal to holiness or sin. "No" has to take place right there before temptation starts. The eyes and ears can influence the mind and heart, but you can turn off your mind and ignore your heart if you want to. That is where temptation comes in, followed by choice and mastering sin. Your decision will come out of your mouth. Listen to what Jesus said about our mouths.

Matthew 12:34-37 You brood of vipers, how can you who are evil say anything good? For out of the overflow of the heart the mouth speaks. The good man brings good things out of the good stored up in him, and the evil man brings evil things out of the evil stored up in him. But I tell you that men will have to give an account on the day of judgment for every careless word they have spoken. For by your words you will be acquitted, and by your words you will be condemned."

You can live a life full of good, you can live a life full of nothingness, or you can sabotage yourself by filling your heart with evil. It starts with what you set before your eyes and ears and allow into your heart. Make no mistake; the enemy wants to store his lies in your heart. Sometimes feelings lie. That's why we have to guard our hearts. Whatever you allow to settle in your heart, will manifest itself in your personality. Here's the good thing; your heart can be cleaned up like a messy room. You are not stuck with a rotten heart. We serve an awesome God don't we! God made us that way. We are His perfect design. God's true love is our freedom of choice to do God's will or our own will. God will not force His way into our hearts. We must choose to store Him there. We do that by keeping the Word continually before our eyes. That is how God becomes your friend. He's not afraid of the things in our hearts that need to be cleaned up. He loves us so much that when we ask Him, He steps in and helps us clean up the mess. He will always say yes when we ask for help. The Word tells us that God searches our hearts. You cannot hide what is in your heart from God. He doesn't have to wait for something in our hearts to manifest itself before He knows it's there. He goes straight to our heart and searches it to see what we have stored there. Notice in the following verses, the heart and the mind are connected. They affect each other. The heart and mind directly affect our conduct and motives.

Jeremiah 17:10 I the Lord search the heart and examine the mind to reward a man according to his conduct, according to what his deeds deserve.

1 Chronicles 28:9(b) For the Lord searches every heart and understands every motive behind the thoughts....

1 Samuel 16:7 But the Lord said to Samuel, "Do not consider his appearance or his height, for I have rejected him. The Lord does not look at the things man looks at. Man looks at the outward appearance but the Lord looks at the heart."

The leaders of Israel died along with all the Israelites who had experienced and seen with their own eyes all the things God had done. There was no leadership left who could remind the people to obey God. Everything had been recorded in the Book of the Law but the people were not reading it anymore. God told them to read it every day and tell their children and their children's children when they get up and lie down and wherever they go. God gave them joyful celebrations to observe so they would remember. Talk about what God has done morning and night. The surrounding nations sure did. Rahab said it all (Joshua 2). They didn't see what God had done, but they sure heard about it. Rahab said their hearts melted and their courage failed because of what they heard about Israel and their God. They were all talking about it and there was no doubt in Rahab's mind about who the real God was. She stored all those stories in her heart and her heart fed her mind and her mind dictated her actions. No other nation had a king who did the things Israel's God did. You would think that those nations would have come over to God's side like Rahab did.

God said to fix His words in our hearts and minds; attach them so they will stay there. Write them on the doorframes of your houses and on your gates so that they are forever before your eyes. The Israelites set up piles of rocks everywhere they went as monuments to remind them of God's mercy, wrath, deliverance and blessings. They put up visible reminders of what God had done for them in that place so they wouldn't forget when they passed by again. But you can't just leave the reminders and never talk about why they are there or else you just have piles of rocks that mean nothing because everyone forgot. You have to read and talk about what God has done. That will make you remember to keep his commandments and trust in Him. If we don't remember what God has done and store that in our hearts, Satan will try and fill our hearts with his junk and we will fall.

What do you have your eyes set on? What do you set before your eyes? What do your eyes and ears feed your mind and fill your heart with that causes your mouth and feet and hands to act? Do your eyes and ears feed your faith so that when trouble comes

50

you are ready to do battle? Do you protect your eyes and ears from seeing and hearing things that will cause you to stumble? God had a great idea about this.

Numbers 15:37-41 The Lord said to Moses, "Speak to the Israelites and say to them: 'Throughout the generations to come you are to make tassels on the corners of your garments, with a blue cord on each tassel. You will have these tassels to look at and so you will remember all the commands of the Lord, that you may obey them and not prostitute yourselves by going after the lusts of your own hearts and eyes. Then you will remember to obey all my commands and will be consecrated to your God. I am the Lord your God, who brought you out of Egypt to be your God. I am the Lord your God.'"

To be consecrated means the same thing as to be sanctified. You are to be set-apart for God. You belong to Him. You are not like the other nations. The tassels are so you will look at them and remember the mighty things God has done for you. They are to keep you from sinning. Think about this for a minute. There are four corners to a garment, two in front and two in back. There are over a million people. All the tassels have a blue cord in common. The tassel itself might be different colors, but the cord had to be blue. If everyone wore all four tassels, there would be more than four million tassels running around the camp. There were tassels everywhere! Even if you forgot to put yours on, you couldn't help but see someone else's. If you were about to sin you would see a tassel and reconsider. Look at the tassels and remember God's commands, that you may obey them and that God is the one who brought you out of Egypt; He is the Lord your God. We have to remember here that the Israelites were surrounded on all sides in their camp by the supernatural protection of God Himself and still they had to be reminded to obey. How much harder is it for you to remember God if you live in the enemies camp where there are no reminders? After a while, you become blind to sin and God.

Jeremiah 6:15 Are they ashamed of their loathsome conduct? No, they have no shame at all; they do not even know how to blush. So they will fall among the fallen; they will be brought down when I punish them," says the Lord

Remembering what God has said and done is so important that God said to wear tassels. They could feel the tassels hit their legs and see them on the garments of others so they would remember. If you see tassels everywhere and God's words are written on your doorframes and gates so that you see them when you come and go and everyone everywhere is talking about what God has done morning and night, how could you forget to obey? Beautiful! We should still wear tassels because God said "throughout the generations" and we are children of Abraham after all. It certainly wouldn't hurt.

Ephesians 3:6 This mystery is that through the gospel the Gentiles are heirs together with Israel, members together of one body, and sharers together in the promise in Christ Jesus.

Incredibly, Israel forgot. Impossible. The celebrations had stopped. There were no more tassels. Nobody was talking about the Deliverer. Faith was gone and now Israel wants a king (1 Samuel 8). Everyone else had a king. The Israelites set their eyes on the kings of the nations around them and now they wanted one too. The elders of Israel said to Samuel, "Give us a king to lead us like all the other nations have." Even the elders had fallen out of relationship with God. Samuel was the last of the faithful. He set his sons as judges but they were crooks, and did not follow in his footsteps, and now the elders are asking for a king. Samuel was displeased and prayed to the Lord and the Lord told Samuel to do it, but warn the people first what the king would do to them. The king wouldn't love them like God did. The people refused to listen to Samuel and said, "No! We want a king over us. Then we will be like all the other nations, with a king to lead us and to go out before us and fight our battles." They wanted to look like the world. They wanted leadership they could see with their eyes. The King of Kings and Lord of Lords would no longer do-even though everything they wanted in a physical king was exactly what God had been doing for them all along.

"I will take you as my own people and I will be your God." (Exodus 6:7)
"We want a king!"
"You are my treasured possession. You are for me a kingdom of priests and a holy nation." (Exodus 19:5-6)
"We want a king!"
"I am the Lord who heals you." (Exodus 15:26)
"We want a king!"
"I will rain down bread from heaven for you." (Exodus 16:4)
"We want a king!"
"I am the Lord your God." (Exodus 20:2)
"We want a king!"
"I will send my terror ahead of you and throw into confusion every nation you encounter. I will make all your enemies turn their backs and run." (Exodus 23:27)
"We want a king!"
"I will love you and bless you and increase your numbers." (Deuteronomy 7:13)
"No! We want a king over us. Then we will be like all the other nations, with a king to lead us and to go out before us and fight our battles." (1 Samuel 8:19-20)
"Listen to them and give them a king." (1 Samuel 8:22)

It was absolutely heart wrenching. They rejected God as their king so God told Samuel to anoint Saul king over Israel. Was God shocked at all this? No. He knew it was coming. Back in Deuteronomy 17:14-20, Moses told the people the rules for the king they would later ask for. One of the rules was that the king himself had to write the entire law on a scroll and read it every day of his life. He was not to turn from the law to the right or to the left. Do you read your Bible every day? Do you set the Word of God before your eyes every day? Are you building a relationship with your Creator? Do you call God your best friend? Can you see the parallel between God and the king and the people of Israel compared to you being the leader of your family and what you should do? Your family is like a miniature nation for God. Your eyes should be in the Word every day so you can be the spiritual leader in your family.

Deuteronomy 17:18 When he takes the throne of his kingdom, he is to write for himself on a scroll a copy of this law, taken from that of the priests, who are Levites. It is to be with him, and he is to read it all the days of his life so that he may learn to revere the Lord his God and follow carefully all the words of this law and these decrees....

1 Samuel 10:25 Samuel explained to the people the regulations of the kingship. He wrote them down on a scroll and deposited it before the Lord. Then Samuel dismissed the people, each to his own home.

Israel could have her king like everyone else, but it stopped there. The regulations were read to both the king and the people so, the people should have kept the king in check. The king was not to take the place of God. He was to lead the people the same way Moses did. Just because they had a king didn't mean they didn't have to obey God. The job of the king was to lead the people in the way of the Lord; same rules, laws, decrees. The only difference was that now they could feast their eyes on a physical king. But here is the problem. It created a faith shift. The faith of the people turned from the Living God they could not see; to the king they could see. That is bad enough. But when the king's eyes are not on God either, you have mayhem. It was the job of the king to feed the people God's Word so that their hearts would trust God and their faith would be in their Creator who delivers. The king was to set the example. When it is a lack of your own faith that gets you in trouble, you failed. When your faith in your king lets you down, he failed. Now you not only have a faith shift, you also have a blame shift. You have someone other than yourself to point the finger at. That is very convenient. "God, our king let us down. Our leadership let us down. Our president let us down. My parents let me down. My spouse let me down. My church let me down. My boss let me down. My friends let me down. My dog let me down. The person or thing I was hoping in instead of you Lord, let me down and I fell."

Israel's first king was Saul. Saul started out OK. But it didn't last long. He took his eyes off of God and fell, taking the people with him. So God rejected him as king and Samuel anointed David instead.

When we read the story of David and Goliath (1 Samuel 17) we see that the Israelites are focused on the Philistines side of the valley. That was the problem. They were completely focused on Goliath. Their eyes were stuck on the problem because the problem looked so big and it had moved fear into their hearts. Too bad the Philistines didn't have tassels on! Maybe the Israelites would have remembered their father God when they saw the tassels.

God is always bigger than the problem. That's why God tells us to keep our eyes on Him. We don't have to see that; we just have to know it. Our eyes need to be fixed on the memory of what He has already done for us. Our perception of God is not limited to what He might look like or how big He is or isn't because we don't know. But we do know what He has done and what He said in His Word. That is what God wants us to see. We have what He has already done planted in our minds and what God has done is not just big, it is huge! Everything else looks so small in comparison. That is why God told Israel that the king should not acquire great numbers of horses for himself and not accumulate large amounts of silver and gold (Deuteronomy 17:16). If you don't have the stuff, your eyes are free to focus on and trust in what is stored in your heart. They have nowhere else to go except on your Deliverer. When God is on your side, you don't need to depend upon the stuff.

55

Deuteronomy 20:1-4 When you go to war against your enemies and see horses and chariots and an army greater than yours, do not be afraid of them, because the Lord your God, who brought you up out of Egypt will be with you. When you are about to go into battle, the priest shall come forward and address the army. He shall say: "Hear O Israel, today you are going into battle against your enemies. Do not be fainthearted or afraid; do not be terrified or give way to panic before them. For the Lord your God is the one who goes with you to fight for you against your enemies to give you victory."

That was the rule for going to war that God gave Moses for the people. The priest would address the army and give them the words of God. Don't worry about what you see because God is bigger and He will give you the victory. Your enemies have their stuff, but you don't need any stuff to haul around because you have your God to fight your battles for you. Remember what God did for you before.

Psalm 33:16-18 No king is saved by the size of his army; no warrior escapes by his great strength. A horse is a vain hope for deliverance; despite all its great strength it cannot save. But the eyes of the Lord are on those who fear Him, on those whose hope is in his unfailing love.

But Samuel is not in charge anymore, Saul is. Saul should have been the one to go in front of the people and remind them and encourage them and give them God's victory speech. But Israel's knowledge of God's greatness had waned. They had no relationship with God and the people didn't know what to do. They were totally dependent on their earthly king and their earthly king had no idea what to do either. The Spirit of the Lord had departed from Saul because of his disobedience, and he had become like a useless idol to Israel. Now the Philistines are on one hill and the Israelites are on another. Israel is completely focused on big Goliath and all of his great big stuff, and they are totally dependent on Saul to deliver them. Satan had filled Israel's eyes with his stuff and their eyes and ears fed their minds so that their hearts were terrified of what their eyes and ears were seeing and hearing. The memory of what God had done for them was gone.

Goliath comes out of the Philistine camp and declares himself a Philistine and says, "Are you not the servants of Saul?" Ouch!!! What happened to the servants of the Living God? That is how they used to be known. Goliath was just calling it like all the Philistines were seeing it. In the eyes of the Philistines, Israel's God had disappeared, so they were not afraid anymore. Worse yet, Israel proves it by not saying anything back. The nation that was once terrified of Israel's God is now daring Israel to fight them. And instead, on hearing Goliath's words, now it is Saul and all the Israelites who are dismayed and terrified. They should have been furious with the Philistines for messing with them. This went on twice a day for forty days. Never in all that time are we told that Israel remembered their God and cried out to Him for help. Their eyes were on Goliath and their hope in Saul. Saul put his hope back into the people that one of them would come out and fight, and he even offered a prize for it, ridiculous. They had forgotten their God who delivers. It could have been over before it began.

Now here comes our hero David. David hadn't forgotten his God. He had already been anointed king over Israel. The only ones who know are his family and Samuel. When he was anointed, the Holy Spirit came upon him in power. His heart was totally filled with God's stuff. God and David were friends. Now he is loaded down with grain, bread and cheese. Not exactly the stuff of a warrior. David's battle supplies were stored in his heart waiting for an opportune time. The Bible says that when David got there, Goliath came out and started bellowing his usual rhetoric. Only this time, David heard it and he saw Israel run in great fear. In just two sentences, David sizes up both Goliath and Israel. It is so good you have to read it yourself.

1 Samuel 17:26 David asked the men standing near him, "What will be done for the man who kills this Philistine and removes this disgrace from Israel?   Who is this uncircumcised Philistine that he should defy the armies of the living God?"

David starts by asking what the reward is for getting rid of Goliath because he already knows the reward is his! Right away David recognized Goliath as a disgrace in Israel and it makes him mad. He absolutely nails it. He says out loud in the hearing of everyone around him, "Who does this guy, who is not in the covenant, think he is to stand in front of the army of the living God and spew insults at them? Why have you allowed this to go on for so long, Israel, and why did you run? You are the army of the living God. Why are you not mad? The God of Israel is alive! Goliath should be very afraid of you and your God."

David is reminding Israel of who they are and David's brother Eliab gets mad at him for it.   He calls David an insignificant shepherd, conceited and wicked.   Really Eliab is probably embarrassed that he didn't come up with it first. Righteous indignation makes you press on, so David turned to another group and said the same thing.   That is where divine intervention entered in, because the right person heard it and went and told Saul and Saul sent for David. David was God's tool of choice because David could be trusted with the God stuff stored in his heart.

When you are where you are supposed to be spiritually, God will orchestrate events for His glory because He can trust you to get His job done. It doesn't matter how old you are. God sent David because he knew his heart was right. David tells Saul not to be afraid of the Philistine and that he will fight him. Saul doesn't get it yet, so he compares David to Goliath in size and ability. Do you get it? Saul still has problems with his eyes. Saul sees the problems and David hears the insults. What David saw in Goliath was a non-issue. What he saw in Israel was their living God. David's God was way bigger than the Philistines.

God hadn't forgotten the Israelites. He had been building up David's faith for this very moment by using the lion and the bear.

58

God and David had been practicing together! David recognized the counterfeit right away and there was no fear in him. David tells Saul that the Lord who delivered him from the lion and the bear will deliver him from the hand of the Philistine. That is how you prophesy. You speak your faith out loud and tell the situation how it is going to be according to the Word of God. David is telling Saul what God has already done and that He will do it again.

1 Samuel 17:36-37 Your servant has killed both the lion and the bear; this uncircumcised Philistine will be like one of them, because he has defied the armies of the living God. The Lord who delivered me from the paw of the lion and the paw of the bear will deliver me from the hand of this Philistine."

David tells Saul that God will deliver him from Goliath. You don't defy the people of God and not pay the price. He doesn't take the credit for the lion, bear, or the victory over Goliath. Saul says "Go, and the Lord be with you." Maybe David's story of the lion and the bear finally reminded Saul of his God. He still tried to give David his armor, but it didn't fit and David didn't need it anyway. So David the shepherd went to battle with his rock.

For forty days, twice a day, Goliath had challenged Israel to a fight. Now, after forty days here comes a kid with a staff and a slingshot–unbelievable. They are both coming off a hill, so Goliath, with his shield bearer in front of him, has to get a little closer to notice that David is just a boy. It's not like David is being forced by Israel to do this. Israel was probably just as shocked as Goliath was. He approaches Goliath and the shield bearer alone. The Bible says Goliath despised David. He hated him. How embarrassing for him to have to fight a child in front of Israel and the Philistines. This is not what he had in mind. He was looking for Israel's mightiest warrior to take down. He wanted something that would build up his reputation and make him look good.

Who does Israel send: a kid. A shocked Goliath is the first one to speak.

1 Samuel 17:43-44 He said to David, "Am I a dog, that you come at me with sticks?" And the Philistine cursed David by his gods. "Come here," he said, "and I'll give your flesh to the birds of the air and the beasts of the field!"

Goliath was prophesying too, but the problem was that he prophesied by himself. His victory would be the result of his own efforts. He, Goliath, would be the one to defeat David, and he cursed David by gods that don't exist. His prophecy was powerless.

David was undaunted. Goliath's words hit David's shield of faith, and it quenched all the fiery darts of the devil. Picture the windshield of a car with bugs hitting it as you drive along. You don't really notice the bugs hitting it because you are so used to the protection of the windshield. You have so much faith in the windshield to keep the bugs off you that you don't even think about it anymore. If the bug is a really big one that makes a loud noise, you might be startled for a moment. But you remember how glad you are that the windshield is there and you forget about it and go on.

The King of Kings and Lord of Lords, the Deliverer of Israel, Ancient of Days, the Great I Am was David's windshield. Not one of Goliath's ugly words got past David's eyes or ears into his heart. They didn't come near his mind because his mind was being fed by what he had stored in his heart. His heart was so stuffed with God's stuff there wasn't room for Goliath's stuff. His mind was on what God had already done and what God was going to do that day and he prophesied too.

1 Samuel 17:45-47 David said to the Philistine, "You come against me with sword and spear and javelin, but I come against you in the name of the Lord Almighty, the God of the armies of Israel, whom you have defied. This day the Lord will hand you over to me, and I'll strike you

60

down and cut off your head. Today I will give the carcasses of the Philistine army to the birds of the air and the beasts of the earth and the whole world will know that there is a God in Israel. All those gathered here will know that it is not by sword or spear that the Lord saves; for the battle is the Lord's, and he will give all of you into our hands."

David's prophesy was all encompassing. It was directed not just to Goliath, but to Israel and the Philistine army, too. David reminded everyone who the God of Israel was, what would happen that day and who would do it. God would hand Goliath over to David. It was not by David's own strength. He mocked Goliath by using Goliath's own words back on him. It wouldn't be just Goliath who fell that day, but the whole Philistine army. Their carcasses would not be fed to the beasts in that field only, but to the beasts of the earth. And the best thing, the whole world will know that there is a God in Israel. Faith makes you see the big picture. The battle was the Lord's. Israel may have forgotten God, but God did not forget them. Goliath would get his mighty warrior, but never in his wildest dreams did he think it would turn out like this. How fitting that a child would show Israel the way.

1 Samuel 17:48-49 As the Philistine moved closer to attack him, David ran quickly toward the battle line to meet him. Reaching into his bag and taking out a stone, he slung it and struck the Philistine on the forehead. The stone sank into his forehead, and he fell face down on the ground.

What was a battle line for David was a fence line for Goliath. David didn't move carefully, slowly, cautiously toward the battle line. He ran quickly! He didn't give fear an opportunity. The outcome had already been decided; now it just needed to be finished. God worked just as fast and suddenly it was done. Can you imagine the mayhem that followed? Everything switched. Now it was the Philistines who were terrified and ran. Israel and Judah surged forward with a shout and ran after the Philistines.

The outcome was exactly what David had said it would be. He struck down Goliath and cut off his head. Then Israel conquered the Philistines and plundered their camp and the whole world knew who the God of Israel was. More than three thousand years have gone by and we are still talking about it.

David would have to learn much more before he could became a king and lead a nation. Like David and Joseph before him, God will use you where you are if you are living according to His Word. He will start out small and as you grow, He will trust you with bigger things if you are faithful. You cannot be double minded doing one thing and saying another.

James 1:5-8 If any of you lacks wisdom, he should ask God, who gives generously to all without finding fault, and it will be given to him. But when he asks, he must believe and not doubt, because he who doubts is like a wave of the sea, blown and tossed by the wind. That man should not think he will receive anything from the Lord; he is a double-minded man, unstable in all he does.

James 4:7-8 Submit yourselves, then, to God. Resist the devil, and he will flee from you. Come near to God and he will come near to you. Wash your hands, you sinners, and purify your hearts, you double-minded.

When you don't have a relationship with God, you have one with the enemy. You have the choice to choose one or the other. You can't be neutral towards both because neutrality towards God is allegiance to Satan. That is just how it works. God wants your whole heart so He can show you his mercy and love and in the end, scoop you up in His arms and take you to heaven to live with Him forever. We can all be David. It is a heart condition based on obeying God.

Israel left her first love and melded into the world. Everything the enemy put in front of Israel's eyes drew her away from God because she quit looking at God's things. She didn't love God anymore. She loved the things of the world. She went after Satan's lies instead. The things God said "no" to no longer mattered. They were all right now because everyone around them was doing the same thing: sexual immorality, drunkenness, idol worship, forgetting the Sabbath and marrying into other nations. What a relief to not be under the law anymore. That is until they got into trouble and needed God to deliver them.

It is the same thing today. You went to church and heard the gospel. But you allowed your eyes to wander and rested them a little too long on the world's stuff. Now living in sin, sexual immorality, marrying unequally yoked, homosexuality, swearing, drunkenness, drugs, nudity, idol worship and the same things that Israel did are no problem for you either. And like Israel, you will need God to bail you out sooner or later because you are not obeying the Lord, and that always brings on trouble and distress.

Numbers 15:30-31 "'But anyone who sins defiantly, whether native-born or alien, blasphemes the Lord, and that person must be cut off from his people. Because he has despised the Lord's word and broken his commands, that person must surely be cut off; his guilt remains on him.' "

Romans 2:5-11 But because of your stubbornness and your unrepentant heart, you are storing up wrath against yourself for the day of God's wrath, when his righteous judgment will be revealed. God "will give to each person according to what he has done." To those who by persistence in doing good seek glory, honor and immortality he will give eternal life. But for those who are self-seeking and who reject the truth and follow evil, there will be wrath and anger. There will be trouble and distress for every human being who does evil: first for the Jew, then for the Gentile; but glory, honor and peace for everyone who does good: first for the Jew, then for the Gentile. For God does not show favoritism.

Your spirit inside you is starving for God. That's the emptiness you feel inside even though you think you have it all. The thing that is missing is the Holy Spirit, and he will not share your heart with the things of the world. You need to repent and stop doing the things that grieve God. Then you will truly have it all.

Isaiah 7:4a Say to him, "Be careful, keep calm and don't be afraid. Do not lose heart"....

Isaiah 7:9b "If you do not stand firm in your faith, you will not stand at all."

That's what God told Isaiah to say to Ahaz before he went into battle against his enemies. That is what we should do, too, when we face difficult situations.

God has given us His Word so we will take the time to remember Him. Then when problems arise, we can say, "My God is bigger than this. My faith is in my Deliverer." Are you and God practicing together? Fill your eyes and your heart with God's Word every day so God can use you. The God-stuff you have stored in your heart goes with you everywhere so you are always ready. Then you can run confidently into battle with your Rock.

Chapter 3
What Does the Army of God Look Like

2 Chronicles 16:9a
For the eyes of the Lord range throughout the earth to strengthen those
whose hearts are fully committed to Him.

When the world looks at you, what do they see? Do you look different to the unsaved world or do you kind of match them a little? According to the Bible we are a chosen people, a royal priesthood, a holy nation, a people belonging to God (1 Peter 2:9). We are aliens and strangers in this world, sanctified, set apart, made holy. We are in this world, but we are not of it. We are to declare the praises of Him who called us out of darkness into His wonderful light. We are to be blameless before Him. The eyes of God actually search around the earth to find those whose hearts are fully committed to Him so He can show Himself strong to them. Is that you?

Do you call yourself a Christian? Are you a follower of Christ, believer in God, saved, sanctified, justified, redeemed and bound for glory but living to the contrary? Do you think the rules have changed because the world has changed? What was not acceptable back in that day is acceptable now because, well, we have evolved, and God is a nice god and loves us no matter what we do? Besides, Jesus died on the cross so all my sins are covered anyway.

Some of you were born and raised in church. You have read the Bible or parts of it. You had Godly parents, went to all the meetings and heard all the good speakers. You call yourself a "Christian" and you hang out with "Christian" friends. Maybe your family was not Christian and you got saved as an adult. Whoever you are, whatever your situation is you have compromised with the world or you are thinking about compromising and your salvation is on the line because of it.

There are lifestyles that you choose to live in day-by-day that will eliminate blessings from your life and keep you from heaven. They will render you lifeless and powerless and without joy because the fruit of the Holy Spirit is gone. You know the Bible says they are wrong, but you choose to do them anyway. The Bible calls this "presumptuous (willful) sin." It is called a "great transgression." Why are you not afraid?

Psalm 19:13 Keep your servant also from willful sins; may they not rule over me. Then will I be blameless, innocent of great transgression.

The lack of the "fear of the Lord" in your life means the Lord is not "in" your life. You have left God out. The flesh man has overcome the spirit man and what is left is a soul bound for hell because heaven has been rejected, and when you cry, "Lord, Lord" He will say, "Depart from me, I never knew you." What happened? Was your first love never really your first love?

Did you learn somewhere along the way that cheap grace would carry you along until you eventually got it together? Once saved, always saved? Do you think that if you sin for a while, there will be time to be good later? After all, you gave your life to Christ a long time ago. He will forgive you anyway. Your name is still written in the Lamb's Book of Life, right? If you die in the middle of your mess, you will still go to heaven, right? Will you, are you sure? Who have you damaged along the way? Who sees your lifestyle and knows you go to church and labels Christians "hypocrites" because of it, if you still go to church at all.

When the Bible says *"All things work together for good for those who love Him and are called according to His purpose" (Romans 8:28),* it is talking about every one of us. We are all called to love Him. Every human on the planet is supposed to go to heaven. That is the love of God. Our salvation is a heart condition. We go to hell because we reject His Son, Jesus, and the work He did on the cross. You reject the cross when you sin. The blood covers the sin and sanctifies you when you accept Christ. You reject Christ when you don't live a sanctified life. Your lifestyle will tell your story. How you live your life will display your heart condition to the world. You are not free to sin because you are saved. You are saved by faith in Jesus, and because of that you reject sin and love the Father, Son and Holy Spirit more than the things of the world. You have been sanctified, set apart and made holy.

1 Peter 2:9-10 (KJV) But ye are a chosen generation, a royal priesthood, an holy nation, a peculiar people; that ye should shew forth the praises of him who hath called you out of darkness into his marvelous light; Which in time past were not a people, but are now the people of God: which had not obtained mercy, but now have obtained mercy.

1 Peter 2:11-12 (NIV) Dear friends, I urge you, as aliens and strangers in the world, to abstain from sinful desires, which war against your soul. Live such good lives among the pagans that, though they accuse you of doing wrong, they may see your good deeds and glorify God on the day he visits us.

We are strangers and aliens in this world. As Christians we are not supposed to look like the world. We are "in" the world but we are not "of" the world. It's cool to be peculiar for Jesus. You may not think so, but it is attractive to the world because of the Holy Spirit in you.

Do you realize how Israel must have looked to the nations around them as they were on their way to Canaan? There were over a million Israelites when they left Egypt. That is a lot of people. The Bible says they left Egypt armed for battle and an angel of God was in front of them. A pillar of cloud led them by day and a pillar of fire by night. The nations around them could see all this as Israel passed by.

The Israelites were on their way to Canaan. When they got to the Red Sea, Pharaoh changed his mind and sent his whole army and all his chariots and all his horses after them (Exodus 14). The Israelites got to the sea and couldn't go any further. They looked back and there are the Egyptians coming after them. They were terrified! Your spiritual eyes should trump your physical eyes, but the relationship between the Israelites and God was new. They had been in bondage for 430 years and forgot their Deliverer. They were learning to trust in Him all over again. Now God lets them physically see their deliverance and the angel of God and the pillar of cloud get in between them. On the Egyptians side it is dark and on Israel's side it is light. It stays like that all night so they don't go near each other. In the meantime, God is driving the sea back with a strong wind and turning the ground beneath the sea into dry land with a wall of water on the right and left. Talk about supernatural! It was light on the Israelites side. They were watching all this. What did that sound like?

The Israelites go through the sea on dry ground with Pharaoh's army hot on their trail. The Army is getting closer and closer so God causes the Egyptians to go into confusion and makes the wheels of their chariots fall off. The Egyptians were terrified and said, "Let's get away from the Israelites! The Lord is fighting for them against Egypt." But it was too late. The Israelites were already across and at daybreak God caused the waters to go back into place and cover up the entire army of Egypt that had followed the Israelites into the sea. The Bible says that not one of them survived and Israel saw them lying dead on the shore. What a night! Can you imagine how word must have spread like wildfire?

King: "Hey Pharaoh, can you help us take that city over there?"

Pharaoh: "Nope."

King: "What do you mean, "Nope"?

Pharaoh: "Got no army."

King: "What do you mean you, 'got no army'"?

Pharaoh: "Drowned."

King: "What?"

Pharaoh: "We had a problem with frogs, gnats, flies, boils, hail, locusts, darkness and our firstborn...."

So word gets around about this strange new nation that has a God who protects them in supernatural ways.

Israel was not just a noisy tangled mass of people camping together on their way to a new home. They were magnificent! There was order in the camp because God is a God of order. He told them how He wanted them to travel and they obeyed God. They marched by tribe, and each tribe had their place in the order. The Levites led the procession with the Ark of the Covenant. But that's not all. There was the pillar of cloud before them by day and the pillar of fire by night so they could travel day or night (Exodus 13:21-22, 40:38). When they stopped, the tabernacle was set up in the center and the tribes of Israel camped in order around it, each with their standards and banners (Numbers 2:1-2). That means they had signs and flags in front of each tribe to distinguish them one from another. The cloud covered the tent of meeting and the glory of the Lord filled the tabernacle. Israel would stay where they were until the cloud lifted, and then they would follow it. How cool is that? What a sight! The nations around them could see this. They were a traveling city being led by an angel of God and the supernatural followed them wherever they went. Every city they came in contact with was touched by the supernatural events of the Israelite's God. That is your God.

69

That is whom you serve. You should look different, act different and be different. The supernatural should be a way of life for you, not just something you read about in the Bible. You should have a godly reputation that sets you apart and draws others to you because of the Holy Spirit inside you.

Do you remember the story of Balaam in the Old Testament (Numbers 22)? He was the pagan prophet summoned by Balak, King of Moab, to curse the Israelites. The Israelites were camped outside of Moab and King Balak was terrified because there were so many of them. He said, "They came out of Egypt and they are large and powerful." Israel had quite a reputation. King Balak heard about Israel's deliverance from Egypt and the cities they destroyed. He saw what Israel had done to his neighbors the Amorites when they wouldn't let Israel pass through their territory (Numbers 21). Now more than a million Israelites were camped in the plains of Moab by the Jordan River. King Balak could see Israel's huge numbers and he was filled with dread because he thought Moab was next on Israel's hit list. The people of Moab were freaking out! They said to the elders of Midian, "This horde is going to lick up everything around us, as an ox licks up the grass of the field."

Instead of allowing Israel to just pass through, King Balak decided to defeat them by using sorcery. Fear causes you to do desperate acts. He thought he would use spiritual means to defeat Israel because he couldn't defeat them on his own. Israel had a spiritual reputation. As Christians, we are to have a spiritual reputation. So the king hired a sorcerer named Balaam to put a curse on the Israelites. Balaam had a reputation, too. King Balak said, "They cover the face of the land and they are too powerful for me." Christians are to be powerful (strong in the Lord, Ephesians 6:10) and cover the face of the land. So God intervened and came to Balaam and told him he could not curse Israel because they are blessed and to bless Israel instead. As Christians, we are blessed. Israel didn't even know all this was going on. While they were minding their own business, God was

70

protecting them. God specifically told them to leave their brothers the Moabites alone because they were descendants of Lot. The land they were on had been given to Lot by God. It was not for Israel (Deuteronomy 2:9). Israel had no plans against Moab. They were preparing to go into the Promised Land. They were setting themselves up to take Jericho. The Holy Spirit intercedes in behalf of God's people.

We have to take pause here and notice the descendants of Lot. Remember, Lot was with Abraham when God was making Israel a nation way back at the beginning, so Lot knew God. Lot moved out of Abraham's camp and it went downhill from there for him and his family. His daughters bore him children that became the Moabites and the Ammonites, both of whom were enemies of the descendants of Abraham. But God was faithful to Lot and gave him land. Now, hundreds of years later, this is the land the Israelites were now passing through. The Moabites should have known God. They should have welcomed Israel, their relatives, into their land and blessed them. Especially when they saw what happened when other cities treated them badly. If Lot had trained his family in the way of the Lord, his generations would have done better. Maybe they would have been Godly. One back-slider would have the power to influence generations for evil because he was disobedient. On the other hand, one Godly man, Abraham, had the power to change the world for good forever because he was obedient. That's amazing. Now these people are meeting and the King of Moab wants Israel gone. He wants to do it by cursing them, but God is the one in charge, not Balak.

Three times Balaam tells the king he cannot curse Israel. He can only speak what God will allow him to say. God will only allow Balaam to bless Israel. So King Balak decided to sacrifice cattle and sheep. He did what? Satan tries to copy God to deceive the world. He does this by perverting God's ways. The sacrifices of the Israelites were for repentance and atonement for sin. The sacrifices of King Balak were meant for sorcery and evil. The liver and organs were given to Balaam for divination. They were laid

71

on seven altars. Seven is God's number for perfection and completeness. Satan is a thief and a liar. People will copy Christians to try and get what they've got because the Holy Spirit in them is attractive. They don't realize they can have the Holy Spirit, too. Balaks sacrifices didn't work. In Balaam's second blessing he says in *Numbers 23:23 "There is no sorcery against Jacob, no divination against Israel."* Hallelujah! You cannot curse what God has blessed. *No weapon formed against you will prosper (Isaiah 54:17). The gates of hell will not prevail against you (Matthew 16:18).*

King Balak took Balaam to three different locations to view the Israelites. Their numbers were so huge they could not all be seen. In his first blessing of Israel, Balaam said in *Numbers 23:9 "From the rocky peaks I see them; from the heights I view them. I see a people who live apart and do not consider themselves one of the nations."* Israel was *in* this world, but they were not *of* this world. They were beautiful to look at. They were different. As Christians we should look different to the outside world because we are in this world but we are not of it. Listen to part of Balaam's third blessing in Numbers 24:5 *"How beautiful are your tents, O Jacob, your dwelling places, O Israel."* Balaam was not saved. He was a pagan diviner from the east being used by God to bless Israel. God told Balaam he could only say what God would allow him to say. Three times Balaam blessed Israel instead of cursing them as King Balak had asked. Finally King Balak told Balaam not to bless them or curse them at all.

As Christians, we are to be sanctified. That means set apart for God and made holy. We are different. We are supposed to look different, act different, speak different and live different. We are not only blessed, we are called to be a blessing. It is wonderful to be different for God.

The fourth time Balaam prophesied Moab's doom because King Balak tried to curse Israel. God's people are protected. Balaam repeated God's promise to Abraham when he said, "May those who bless you be blessed and those who curse you be cursed!" Moab would be wiped out later for trying to curse Israel, but God's people are a blessed people.

We are to be a salt and a light. Do you understand that is attractive to the world? Balaam in his first blessing (Numbers 23:10) said, *"Let me die the death of the righteous, and may my end be like theirs."* He recognized their righteousness. Righteous means to be right with God. The righteousness of Israel was visible. Your righteousness should be visible to the world. Not a pious righteousness, but a Godly righteousness that sets you apart and makes you different from those around you, because you love God.

Balaam wanted to share in Israel's blessing. That did not happen because salvation is a heart condition, and his heart was bent on evil. Balaam wanted the outward form without the internal substance. I want to look like that, but I don't want to do what it takes to be like that on the inside. He spoke to the one and only living God, the Ancient of Days and yet his heart was unchanged. Astonishing! To Balaam, God was just another deity to be dealt with. He did not know God and had no relationship with Him so he did not recognize God's voice when God spoke to him. Balaam was in the habit of dealing with demons. It did not surprise him that a deity would speak to him. He obeyed out of fear.

After Balaam had blessed Israel three times and prophesied Moab's doom, both he and King Balak turned around and went home. It would be great if the story ended here, but righteousness is about more than just looking good on the outside with standards and banners. Righteousness is about being right with God on the inside as well. It's about your relationship with God. How much do you love Him and how willing are you to obey Him in absolutely everything?

While God was protecting Israel from their enemies, the Israelite men began to mess around with the Moabite woman.

Numbers 25:1-3 While Israel was staying in Shittim, the men began to indulge in sexual immorality with Moabite women, who invited them

73

to the sacrifices to their gods. The people ate and bowed down before these gods. So Israel joined in worshiping the Baal of Peor. And the Lord's anger burned against them.

If you are buried in the world, chances are you did not take your salvation seriously or you never got to know the one who saved you by dying on the cross for your sins. Your salvation was based on someone else's testimony or you just went because your parents did and it was always assumed that you knew the Lord. What is the condition of your heart? Do you love God but love the things of the world, too, so you have a hard time saying no?

1 John 2:15-17 Do not love the world or anything in the world. If anyone loves the world, the love of the Father is not in him. For everything in the world – the cravings of sinful man, the lust of his eyes, and the boasting of what he has and does – comes from the world. The world and its desires pass away, but the one who does the will of God lives forever.

When you were about to make that fence line decision, was there a check in your spirit? Did you stop and consider the blood? Did you wonder what God would think? Did you feel shame, but you chose the other side of the fence anyway? That is rejecting Christ. Or did you just leap over the fence without even thinking about it? That is because the flesh man is bigger than the spirit man. You have spent more time in the world than in God's Word and now you are a part of it without shame. You can't hear from God because your flesh man is louder than your spirit man.

John 8:47 "He who belongs to God hears what God says. The reason you do not hear is that you do not belong to God."

Your spirit is like a muscle. The more you exercise it, the more it grows. You exercise your spirit by spending time with God. You spend time with God by reading His Word. That is how you get to know Him. That is the spiritual protein your spirit muscle is starving for. As you do this you will begin to feel your spirit man rise above your flesh man. You will feel that check in your spirit when you are about to make a wrong decision. You will begin to hear from God. You will find yourself saying "the Lord told me this" and "the Lord told me that." The Lord was always telling you this and that, but you couldn't hear because you were filled with the world and not the Word and the world was more attractive to you.

Matthew 7:7-8 Ask and it will be given to you; seek and you will find; knock and the door will be opened to you. For everyone who asks receives; he who seeks finds; and to him who knocks, the door will be opened.

Hebrews 4:12 For the word of God is living and active. Sharper than any double-edged sword, it penetrates even to dividing soul and spirit, joints and marrow; it judges the thoughts and attitudes of the heart.

2 Timothy 3:16-17 All scripture is God-breathed and is useful for teaching, rebuking, correcting and training in righteousness, so that the man of God may be thoroughly equipped for every good work.

Psalm 18:30 (KJV) As for God, his way is perfect: the word of the Lord is tried: he is a buckler to all those that trust in him.

Give God the first part of every day. This is a first fruits sacrifice. The enemy will make sure you don't have time if you wait. Set your alarm 15 minutes earlier. At first you will be too tired. You will get to bed too late. You won't feel good. Ignore it all and get up. Go to a place you can be alone.

Do you understand repentance? Repentance is not saying "I'm sorry God" over and over. Repentance is a literal turning around and walking the other way. Repentance means you have changed your mind about your sin. Repentance is not only "I'm sorry God," it is also "I will never do this again. Your way is better than my way." Do the opposite of what you were doing that goes against the Word of God. Repent: Do it no more. As soon as you make the decision to turn around, don't look back. You are living for God now.

When the enemy comes against you like a flood, take your sword and run at the enemy with a flood of Word!

Romans 12:2 Do not conform any longer to the pattern of this world, but be ye transformed by the renewing of your mind. Then you will be able to test and approve what God's will is – His good and pleasing and perfect will.

You must renew your mind to be transformed. That means you must fill it with something different than you were filling it with before. The thing you fill it with is the Bible. That is the only way you can test and approve what God's good and pleasing and perfect will is. It is the only way you can get to know and understand God. Have you had enough of being miserable? Would you like to be filled with the fruits of the Holy Spirit every day?

You cannot have both. You cannot have one foot in heaven and one foot in the world. True love is freedom of choice. If you are not careful, God will give you over to your own desires. He is not going to make you quit what you are doing. He will not force you to walk in His way. Instead He says, this is the way, walk in it. From here on it is up to you. You make the choice. Listen to what Jesus tells us in John.

John 15:5-8 I am the vine; you are the branches. If a man remains in me and I in him, he will bear much fruit; apart from me you can do nothing. If anyone does not remain in me, he is like a branch that is thrown away and withers; such branches are picked up, thrown into the fire and burned. If you remain in me and my words remain in you, ask whatever you wish, and it will be given you. This is to my father's glory, that you bear much fruit, showing yourselves to be my disciples.

The word "remain" means stay. Jesus was talking to his disciples. He was telling them that they had to remain in Him or they would be like a branch thrown into the fire. Not only that, they would have to "show" themselves to be His disciples by bearing fruit. The fruit of the Holy Spirit is love, joy, peace, patience, kindness, goodness, faithfulness, gentleness and self-control (Galatians 5:22-23). To bear fruit and glorify God they would need to remain in Him and His words would have to remain in them because the words of Jesus would help them in times of trouble. If you want to remain in Jesus, His words have to remain in you. That is our safety net. Without His Word, you will fall away. Your fruit shows God that you are a disciple of Jesus. It does matter what you do. It is not a "works" salvation where we earn our way to heaven by what we do. But your behavior after you get saved will show God if you are His disciple or not.

2 Peter 1:3-11 His divine power has given us everything we need for life and godliness, through our knowledge of him who called us by his own glory and goodness. Through these he has given us his very great and precious promises, so that through them you may participate in the divine nature and escape the corruption in the world caused by evil desires. For this very reason, make every effort to add to your faith goodness; and to goodness, knowledge; and to knowledge, self-control; and to self-control, perseverance; and to perseverance, godliness; and to godliness, brotherly kindness; and to brotherly kindness, love. For if you possess these qualities in increasing measure, they will keep you from being ineffective and unproductive in your knowledge of our Lord Jesus Christ. But if anyone does not have them, he is near-sighted and blind, and has forgotten that he has been cleansed from his past sins. Therefore, my brothers, be all the more eager to make your calling and election sure. For if you do these things, you will never fall, and you will receive a rich welcome into the eternal kingdom of our Lord and Savior Jesus Christ.

Is your life a mess? Are you staying away from church? Are

you filled with the things of the world? Are you dating unequally yoked? Are you living in sexual immorality? Are you sad or depressed? Are you filled with rage? Are you battling addictions? Do you have issues with bitterness and unforgivness? Do you need healing? Are you hiding something? Do you think that God can't possibly forgive you?

1 John 1:9 (KJV) If we confess our sins he is faithful and just to forgive us our sins and cleanse us from all unrighteousness.

Who do you choose, the way of the world or the way of God? If you live by the Spirit, you will not gratify the desires of the sinful nature (Galatians 5:16). Read all of Galatians, Ephesians, and Titus. Obeying God is a joyful thing. The fruits of the Holy Spirit are what you are to be filled with every day while you are hoping in Christ.

Psalm 25:4-5 Show me your ways, O Lord, teach me your paths; guide me in your truth and teach me for you are God my Savior, and my hope is in you all day long.

Hope – The joyful expectation of things to come. While you are waiting, hope. While you are hoping, be filled with the Holy Spirit. Ask God to fill you with His Holy Spirit every day. You can be filled with joy while you are waiting for your answers. Serving God is not dull. Look up the word "joy" in your concordance in the back of your Bible. Read them all.

Psalm 119:97-100 Oh, how I love your law! I meditate on it all day long. Your commands make me wiser than my enemies, for they are ever with me. I have more insight than all my teachers, for I meditate on your statutes. I have more understanding than the elders, for I obey your precepts.

Joshua 24:14-15 Now fear the Lord and serve him with all faithfulness. Throw away the gods your forefathers worshiped beyond the River and in Egypt, and serve the Lord. But if serving the Lord seems undesirable to you, then choose for yourselves this day whom you will serve, whether the gods your forefathers served beyond the River, or the gods of the Amorites, in whose land you are living. But as for me and my household, we will serve the Lord.

2 Timothy 2:19 Nevertheless, God's solid foundation stands firm, sealed with this inscription: "The Lord knows those who are his," and, "Everyone who confesses the name of the Lord must turn away from wickedness."

What do you look like to the world? Are you different in a good way? Do people want what you've got? Is the fruit of the Holy Spirit evident in your life? Can God trust you with His Word? It is never too late to get it right with God.

Colossians 3:1-10 Since, then, you have been raised with Christ, set your hearts on things above, where Christ is, seated at the right hand of God. Set your minds on things above, not on earthly things. For you died, and your life is now hidden with Christ in God. When Christ, who is your life, appears, then you also will appear with him in glory. Put to death, therefore, whatever belongs to your earthly nature: sexual immorality, impurity, lust, evil desires and greed, which is idolatry. Because of these, the wrath of God is coming. You used to walk in these ways, in the life you once lived. But now you must also rid yourselves of all such things as these: anger, rage, malice, slander, and filthy language from your lips. Do not lie to each other, since you have taken off your old self with its practices and have put on the new self, which is being renewed in knowledge in the image of its Creator.

Separate yourself from the world by the way you live your life. Not because you are better than everyone else, but because you know the truth and it has set you free from the trappings of the world. Change your mind about how you are living so your testimony will draw others to Christ. Bury yourself in God's Word so you will know Him and do what He says so He can recognize you as one of His own when He comes back.

Chapter 4
The Obedient Army at Home

John 14:23-24
Jesus replied, "If anyone loves me, he will obey my teaching. My Father will love him, and we will come to him and make our home with him. He who does not love me will not obey my teaching. These words you hear are not my own; they belong to the Father who sent me."

What does your home life look like to God? Are you different people when you get to church? If your home life were revealed, would you be embarrassed or is your heart perfect towards Him? Do you seek to do the will of the Father in every situation set in front of you every day? Are you teaching your children to do the same?

Matthew 12:50 For whoever does the will of my father in heaven is my brother and sister and mother.

Matthew 7:21 "Not everyone who says to me, 'Lord, Lord,' will enter the kingdom of heaven, but only he who does the will of my Father who is in heaven."

Luke 6:46 "Why do you call me, 'Lord, Lord,' and do not do what I say?"

Romans 2:13 For it is not those who hear the law who are righteous in God's sight, but it is those who obey the law who will be declared righteous.

Genesis 15:6 Abraham believed the Lord and it was credited to him as righteousness.

To be righteous means to be right with God. Righteousness comes by faith. Did you ever wonder why God chose Abraham to carry out His plan? Why did Abraham get all the blessings? It was because God could trust Abraham with His word. Not the written Word because that wasn't around yet. When God spoke to Abraham, Abraham obeyed. God knew His spoken word was safe with Abraham. Abraham knew the way of the Lord and he would command his family and his household to keep it. In doing so they would be blessed with all God had promised them. What did God promise?

Genesis 18:18 Seeing that Abraham shall surely become a great and mighty nation and all the nations of the earth shall be blessed in him.

Hallelujah! The blessing of the nations is Jesus. Jesus came from the line of Abraham. Why did God choose Abraham? The next verse says it all.

Genesis 18:18-19 "Abraham will surely become a great and powerful nation, and all the nations on earth will be blessed through him. For I know him, that he will command his children and his household after him, and they shall keep the way of the Lord to do justice and judgment; that the Lord may bring upon Abraham that which he hath spoken of him."

Do not take that lightly because it tells us exactly what to do to bring about the promises of the Lord. This is so important. Let's read it again. Do not read it quickly.

Genesis 18:18-19 "Abraham will surely become a great and powerful nation, and all the nations on earth will be blessed through him. For I know him, that he will command his children and his household after him, and they shall keep the way of the Lord to do justice and judgment; that the Lord may bring upon Abraham that which he hath spoken of him."

What does God know about you? God said, "I know him. I know that I can trust him to keep My ways and he will teach his family and his whole camp to do the same. My words will follow (remain in) the line of Abraham for generations because he was faithful. My word is safe with him and because of that I can carry out My plan to create a whole new nation with him. I have a plan for Abraham that is going to affect the entire world for the rest of time and I know he won't mess it up. I am going to allow My very own Son to be born in Abraham's bloodline." God would not be able to do what He wanted to do if Abraham would not keep his household in line. The whole camp would have to keep the way of the Lord to bring about the promise given to Abraham.

Genesis 22:18 "Through your offspring all nations on earth will be blessed, because you have obeyed me."

Because of one man's obedience, all the nations on earth would be blessed. One man! What would happen if all of us were obedient? Abraham had the responsibility of teaching his family and his servants and his staff and his entire household, including everybody's children, how to keep the way of the Lord. Abraham didn't have any children of his own, but he still had a houseful. If Abraham did that, the Lord would fulfill His promises to them. It was conditional. But here is something else God said, "I know him, that he will *command* his children and his household." What else would Abraham do? God knew that He could trust Abraham to not just *tell* his children and family, he would *command* them to keep the way of the Lord. It wasn't optional. It was law. They had no choice in the matter. Even the servants had to obey the way of the Lord. They could not bring their foreign gods or pagan traditions into Abraham's camp, so the people and their children would not be influenced by evil. It was God's way or the highway. Why do you think Abraham had to *command* his children and his household to obey God? Because sometimes they didn't want to do it. Why do you think there was "justice and judgment?" Because sometimes they didn't. So there was fair and loving discipline inflicted on them to bring them back in line with God's Word. One rebellious individual in the household had the power to bring down the whole camp if he was not held accountable for his actions. Remember the yeast Jesus talked about?

Matthew 13:33 He told them still another parable: "The kingdom of heaven is like yeast that a woman took and mixed into a large amount of flour until it worked all through the dough."

There is also the yeast of malice. You can spread holiness or you can spread evil.

When the Lord called Abram (before his name was changed to Abraham) He told him to leave his country and people and his father's household and go to another land. Abram's father Terah was an idolater who lived with his family in Haran where the moon-god was worshiped. Abram would need to be separated from the godless influences of his family and the land where they lived, so God called him out. When you are born-again, you are sanctified. You are set apart and made holy for the Master's use. You are called out of the world. You live in the world, but you are not involved in the unholy things of the world anymore. Abram left, but he took his nephew Lot with him. Lot was a part of his father's household and Abram was supposed to leave him behind. This would mean trouble later.

The land could no longer hold them all because their possessions were so great. The herdsman began to argue, so Abram and Lot had to separate (Genesis 13). Lot chose the whole plain of the Jordan and pitched his tent towards Sodom. Not a good idea, Lot. God had called Abram out of a sinful place and now Lot is taking his family back into one. The Bible tells us that the men of Sodom were wicked and sinning greatly against the Lord. It was already a bad place before Lot moved there. If you pitch your tent next to sin, you will become a part of it, and that is exactly what happened to Lot and his family. Lot and his family end up living in Sodom. Why did he do that? Why would he raise his family in such a place?

Things did not go well for Lot in Sodom. There was war and the conquering kings carried off Lot and all of his possessions. Someone escaped and told Abram, and Abram took 318 trained men born in his household and brought them back (Genesis 14). The sins of Sodom and Gomorrah were very great. God told Abram he was going to completely destroy them. Abram interceded for Lot and his family, and God sent two angels to Sodom to get them out. Lot knew they were angels from God. The angels told Lot to get his family out quickly because they were going to destroy the place.

Genesis 19:15-16 With the coming of dawn, the angels urged Lot, saying, "Hurry! Take your wife and your two daughters who are here, or you will be swept away when the city is punished." When he hesitated, the men grasped his hand and the hands of his wife and of his two daughters and led them safely out of the city, for the Lord was merciful to them.

Could it have been any clearer? And yet verse 16 tells us Lot hesitated. Over what, Lot? Was it your stuff and things? The angels had to grab the hands of Lot, his wife and their two daughters and lead them out of the city. When they got out of the city, they were told to run for their lives and not look back and don't stop in the plain.

They may have gotten out of the city, but the city was not out of them. Lot's wife looked back and turned into a pillar of salt. Looking back represented a longing or sadness for the loss of something that God called grievous sin. Lot finally settles with his daughters in a cave in the mountains, but the city is still in him and his daughters, too. Incest took place because there was no fear of the Lord in his daughters. They got their father drunk and another two nations were born, the Moabites and the Ammonites that would be enemies of Abraham's descendants forever.

This is amazing in light of what had happened. Angels drag them out of their home, their mother turned into a pillar of salt and God rains down burning sulfur on their city. They were so far away from God spiritually that even after all these things they were not driven to their knees in repentance. They would have been destroyed along with the city if Abram had not interceded for them (Genesis 18).

Let's go all the way back to the very beginning of the problem. What would have happened if Abram had completely obeyed God and not taken Lot with him? One thing is sure; the Moabites and the Ammonites would have never existed. Your obedience or disobedience never affects just you.

While Lot was living in Sodom, God was making a covenant with Abram. Lot was losing his influence over his family, but the influence that Abram had on his household was absolute. God made a covenant with Abram and changed his name to Abraham. In the covenant, God told Abraham that he would be the father of many nations. But first, God told him, "Walk before Me and be blameless." Obedience is the prerequisite to receiving from God. He would not tell us to be blameless if it were not possible.

Genesis 17: 1-11 When Abram was ninety-nine years old, the Lord appeared to him and said, "I am God Almighty; walk before me and be blameless. I will confirm my covenant between me and you and will greatly increase your numbers."

Abram fell facedown, and God said to him, "As for me, this is my covenant with you: You will be the father of many nations. No longer will you be called Abram; your name will be Abraham, for I have made you a father of many nations. I will make you very fruitful; I will make nations of you, and kings will come from you. I will establish my covenant as an everlasting covenant between me and you and your descendants after you for the generations to come, to be your God and the God of your descendants after you. The whole land of Canaan, where you are now an alien, I will give as an everlasting possession to you and your descendants after you; and I will be their God.

Then God said to Abraham, "As for you, you must keep my covenant, you and your descendants after you for the generations to come. This is my covenant with you and your descendants after, the covenant you are to keep: Every male among you shall be circumcised. You are to undergo circumcision, and it will be the sign of the covenant between me and you.

In verse 13 God said that every male born in Abraham's household or bought with his money must be circumcised. If they were not, they would be cut off from their people because they had broken the covenant. Ishmael would be blessed and would be the father of twelve rulers and made into a great nation, but the everlasting covenant promise would be established with Isaac and his descendants after him.

Genesis 17: 23 On that very day, Abraham took his son Ishmael and all those born in his household or bought with his money, every male in his household, and circumcised them as God had told him.

Instant obedience! That is how Abraham operated. The covenant of circumcision was a sign of Gods covenant with Abraham and his descendants. Not only would they get the land and the blessings, but God would be their God forever and they would serve only Him. It was a promise between God and His people. God would protect and provide. His people would trust and obey, and obey they did. On that very day they were all circumcised.

They were now a covenant people. They were safely under God's wing of provision and protection. Did you notice that Lot didn't get into trouble until he left Abrahams camp? The camp was a safe place with spiritual boundaries. When Lot went to live in Sodom he removed his family from those boundaries and lived among sin and his family fell. Lot did not have to live in Sodom. He and his wife could have gone back to his family in Haran and raised their daughters there.

Genesis 13:12-13 Abram lived in the land of Canaan, while Lot lived among the cities of the plain and pitched his tents near Sodom. Now the men of Sodom were wicked and were sinning greatly against the Lord.

When you live in the enemy's camp, you begin to take direction from the enemy. When sin is in front of your eyes every day, it appears less and less evil. The enemy whispers over and over to you, "There is no God" and you have the audacity to believe it. You believe it because you didn't obey God and keep His Word before your eyes. You have replaced the Ancient of Days with the very one He warned you about; the one that Jesus died to save you from. You are surrounded by the enemy's stuff and you feast your eyes on the ungodly. You were not forced; you chose and now you are sinning greatly against the Lord. You get mad at God because your life is not going well. God's grace is there to bail you out, but only if you choose to repent. You have to move away from Sodom. If you don't, you are going to hell and you have allowed Satan to win. Do you see? There is no difference between the sins of Adam and Eve and the sins of Sodom and Gomorrah and the sins of us. The same snake is behind them all. The same Healer is waiting for us to come back to Him in repentance under the cross of Jesus that offers us a way out. How foolish of us to continue in our sins.

When Lot and his daughters escaped from Sodom, they did not go back to Abraham. They were not a part of the circumcision covenant and they lived outside of the covenant camp. His daughters were unequally yoked and they escaped Sodom alone. God was willing to save Lot's whole family even though Lot was the only righteous one.

Genesis 19:12-14 The two men said to Lot, "Do you have anyone else here—sons-in-law, sons or daughters, or anyone else in the city who belongs to you? Get them out of here, because we are going to destroy this place. The outcry to the Lord against its people is so great that he has sent us to destroy it." So Lot went out and spoke to his sons-in-law, who were pledged to marry his daughters. He said, "Hurry and get out of this place, because the Lord is about to destroy the city!" But his sons-in-law thought he was joking.

As the head of your household, you are responsible for the spiritual leadership of your family. It is absolutely OK for you to "drag" your children to church or make them sit and listen as you read the Bible to them. As the head of your church, you are responsible for the spiritual leadership of your congregation. It is absolutely OK for you to remove sin from your church. The household of Abraham is a pattern for churches and families alike to follow to receive the promises of God. Sin that refuses Godly correction must be dealt with, with justice and judgment according to the way of the Lord.

A new covenant was made for us through the blood of Jesus that replaced circumcision, but the contract is still the same. We must walk before God Almighty and be blameless. God will be our only God and He will look after us and protect us. Our children must be ready to leave and raise families of their own under the same blood covenant so that generation after generation walks blameless before God.

Galatians 3:26-29 You are all sons of God through faith in Christ Jesus, for all of you who were baptized into Christ have clothed yourselves with Christ.   There is neither Jew nor Greek, slave nor free, male nor female, for you are all one in Christ Jesus. If you belong to Christ, then you are Abraham's seed, and heirs according to the promise.

John 8:39b "If you were Abraham's children," said Jesus, "then you would do the things Abraham did."

Did you know that you are Abraham's seed if you belong to Christ? We are part of Abraham's camp. What have we taught our children and our household after us? Have we taught them to keep the way of the Lord? Do we command them to do what the Lord says? Can God trust you with His Word? Do you and your children know the way of the Lord?

Genesis 18:19b. For I know him, that he will command his children and his household after him, and they shall keep the way of the Lord to do justice and judgment; that the Lord may bring upon Abraham that which he hath spoken of him."

When Abraham was very old and ready to get a wife for his son Isaac, he made his chief servant, Eliezer, swear "by the Lord, the God of heaven and the God of earth" that he would not get a wife for his son from the daughters of the Canaanites. Eliezer had to go back to Abraham's own relatives to get a wife for Isaac. It was very important to preserve the bloodline of Abraham for the nation of Israel that God was creating. Two times Abraham told his servant he could not take Isaac back there with him because God brought Abraham out of his family and their land. Abraham would not allow his son to spend any time under ungodly influences. He was protecting the eyes and ears of Isaac. His soon-to-be wife would be removed from an idolatrous family and join her husband serving God under the covenant. Eliezer swore an oath to Abraham that he would obey and on the way Eliezer prayed that God would provide. There was Godly unity in

Abraham's camp and God did provide. Oh that there would be Godly unity in our families and in our churches.

Every ungodly influence had been removed from Abraham's people. God removed Abraham from his father's household because they were idolaters. Lot and his family and his herdsman were separated from Abraham and Lot allowed his family to fall. Hagar and Ishmael were sent away and Hagar got a wife from Egypt for Ishmael. Hagar was an Egyptian and Ismael was of the wrong bloodline. Abraham's sons from his concubines were sent away from Isaac to the east. God knew that their hearts would not be fully devoted to Him.

Is your heart fully devoted to God? Do you follow God in everything or just some things? What kind of influence are you to your family? Do your children know God? Have you consecrated your house and your lives and devoted them to God? What about your church? Is there sin going on that needs to be removed? Does your church know the way of the Lord and are they willing to do justice and judgment so that there is unity in the camp?

Jeremiah 17:10 "I the Lord search the heart and examine the mind, to reward a man according to his conduct, according to what his deeds deserve."

Psalm 119:9-16 How can a young man keep his way pure? By living according to your word. I seek you with all my heart; do not let me stray from your commands. I have hidden your word in my heart that I might not sin against you. Praise be to you O Lord; teach me your decrees. With my lips I recount all the laws that come from your mouth. I rejoice in following your statutes as one rejoices in great riches. I meditate on your precepts and consider your ways. I delight in your decrees; I will not neglect your word.

God created a new nation through Abraham called Israel that was to be an example to the world of the goodness of God. By their obedience to God and His laws, they would be a wise and understanding people. The nations of the world would look at them and see that they were different and that the God of Israel was real and powerful and loving and took good care of His people. The signs and wonders God performed for Israel are so that the whole world will see that the Lord is powerful. None of the gods of other nations could compare. Israel is a visual example of the greatness of God to the world.

Deuteronomy 4:5-6 (Moses speaking) "See, I have taught you decrees and laws as the Lord my God commanded me, so that you may follow them in the land (neighborhood) you are entering to (live in) take possession of it. Observe them carefully, for this will show your wisdom and understanding to the nations (your neighbors), who will hear about all these decrees and say, 'Surely this great nation (household) is a wise and understanding people.'"(Parenthesis mine)

Joshua 4:24 He did this so that all the peoples of the earth might know that the hand of the Lord is powerful and so that you might always fear the Lord your God.

Our God is a mighty God. He is not a "what," He is a "who." The nations around Israel were serving gods they could see made of wood and clay. But the God of Israel, the God of Abraham, Isaac and Jacob, is the living God. They couldn't see Him physically, but His power was evident to everyone.

Deuteronomy 4:7-8 What other nation is so great as to have their gods near them the way the Lord our God is near us whenever we pray to him? And what other nation is so great as to have such righteous decrees and laws as this body of laws I am setting before you today?

Wouldn't you love to see those words on billboards across America? God's laws are alive and righteous. They are precious. They are loving rules from a loving God given as a gift to a special people so that God's blessings could saturate their lives in front of the whole world. The blessings would not only come upon the people, but they would follow them. They weren't just a one-time deal. The blessings were ongoing and permeated every facet of their lives. The blessings were the living, flowing, automatic result of obedience to a loving, living God.

If they messed up, the blessings stopped, but God's grace was so absolute, they could repent and come back to Him and the blessings would flow again. That is because even when the people sinned and stopped loving God, God still loved them. His Word does not change (Deuteronomy 4:29-31).

Here is the thing: Nothing has changed. The condition of the blessings is the same. Our lives can still be saturated with God's blessings if we just obey Him. God does not lie. But rest assured the penalties for sin have not changed either. If it were not for the crucified Christ, the precious blood of Jesus, none of us would be saved.

John 12:44-50 Then Jesus cried out, "When a man believes in me, he does not believe in me only, but in the one who sent me. When he looks at me, he sees the one who sent me. I have come into the world as a light, so that no one who believes in me should stay in darkness. As for the person who hears my words but does not keep them, I do not judge him. For I did not come to judge the world, but to save it. There is a judge for the one who rejects me and does not accept my words; that very word which I spoke will condemn him at the last day. For I did not speak of my own accord, but the Father who sent me commanded me what to say and how to say it. I know that his command leads to eternal life. So whatever I say is just what the Father has told me to say."

John 14:15 "If you love me, you will obey what I command."

John 14:21 Whoever has my commands and obeys them, he is the one who loves me. He who loves me will be loved by my Father, and I, too, will love him and show myself to him.

John 14:23-24 Jesus replied, "If anyone loves me, he will obey my teaching. My Father will love him, and we will come to him and make our home with him. He who does not love me will not obey my teaching.

These words you hear are not my own; they belong to the Father who sent me."

Acts 26:20b Also, I preached that they should repent and turn to God and prove their repentance by their deeds.

You are saved by grace and you prove your salvation by your deeds. Your behavior after you get saved matters. The whole Bible from beginning to end tells us to repent and obey.

Romans 8:9-17 You, however, are controlled not by the sinful nature but by the Spirit, if the Spirit of God lives in you. And if anyone does not have the Spirit of Christ, he does not belong to Christ. But if Christ is in you, your body is dead because of sin, yet your spirit is alive because of righteousness. And if the Spirit of him who raised Jesus from the dead is living in you, he who raised Christ from the dead will also give life to your mortal bodies through his Spirit, who lives in you.
Therefore, brothers, we have an obligation—but it is not to the sinful nature, to live according to it. For if you live according to the sinful nature, you will die; but if by the Spirit you put to death the misdeeds of the body, you will live, because those who are led by the Spirit of God are sons of God. For you did not receive a spirit that makes you a slave again to fear, but you received the Spirit of sonship. And by him we cry, "Abba, Father." The Spirit himself testifies with our spirit that we are God's children. Now if we are children, then we are heirs—heirs of God and co-heirs with Christ, if indeed we share in his sufferings in order that we may also share in his glory.

No matter what kind of home you grew up in, you are responsible for your own salvation. You must make the decision to obey God or not. You have to decide for yourself if you believe Jesus is the Son of God who died for your sins. Then you must live in such a way that Jesus will recognize you when He comes back for His church and you must teach your family to do the same.

Chapter 5
The Mouth of the Army of God

Luke 6:45
The good man brings good things out of the good stored up in his heart,
and the evil man brings evil things out of the evil stored up in his heart.
For out of the overflow of his heart his mouth speaks.

In Deuteronomy we are constantly told to tell our children and grandchildren what the Lord has done. When we tell them, we, too, are hearing it over and over again for ourselves. When we remember what God has told us and what God has done for us by reading His Word, we don't get in half as much trouble. This is what the enemy is trying to snatch. If he can get God out of us, he wins. Did you ever wonder how Satan could get you away from God? That's how. He can't steal it. But he can snatch God's Word out of you by getting you involved in the world so you give it up yourself.

Mark 4:15 Some people are like seed along the path, where the word is sown. As soon as they hear it, Satan comes and takes away the word that was sown in them.

95

One of his favorite tools is your eyes. But another tool is your tongue. The Bible has so much to say about our mouths. Your testimony is in your mouth. It is one of the weapons of your warfare. When you let Satan use your mouth, it keeps you and others away from God.

Matthew 12:34 You brood of vipers. How can you who are evil say anything good? For out of the overflow of the heart the mouth speaks.

Exodus 20:7 You shall not misuse the name of the Lord your God, for the Lord will not hold anyone guiltless who misuses his name.

James 5:12 Above all, my brothers, do not swear — not by heaven or by earth or by anything else. Let your "Yes" be yes, and your "No," no, or you will be condemned.

Matthew 5:35-37 "Again, you have heard that it was said to the people long ago, 'do not break your oath, but keep the oaths you have made to the Lord.' But I tell you, do not swear at all: either by heaven, for it is God's throne; or by the earth, for it is his footstool; or by Jerusalem, for it is the city of the Great King. And do not swear by your head, for you cannot make even one hair white or black. Simply let your 'Yes' be 'Yes,' and your 'No,' 'No'; anything beyond this comes from the evil one."

Whatever you have stored in your heart will come out of your mouth. If your heart is full of God's Word, God's Word will come out of your mouth. Your character mirrors what is in your heart. It just happens. Why? Because you believe what is in your heart. Be careful what you store in your heart. When Jesus comes back He has a sword in His mouth. Listen carefully because this is powerful.

Revelation 19:11 I saw heaven standing open and there before me was a white horse, whose rider is called Faithful and True. With justice he judges and makes war. His eyes are like blazing fire, and on his head are many crowns. He has a name written on him that no one knows but he himself. He is dressed in a robe dipped in blood and his name is the Word of God. The armies of heaven were following him, riding on white horses and dressed in fine linen, white and clean. Out of his mouth comes a sharp sword with which to strike down the nations. He will rule them with an iron scepter. He treads the winepress of the fury of the wrath of God Almighty. On his robe and on his thigh he has this name written: KING OF KINGS AND LORD OF LORDS.

2 Thessalonians 2:8 And then the lawless one will be revealed, whom the Lord Jesus will overthrow with the breath of his mouth and destroy by the splendor of his coming.

That sword in the mouth of Jesus is the Word of God. He will strike down the nations with the Word of God. Wars are fought and won in the mouth with God's Word. If the sword had been in His hand, it would have meant something different entirely. The sword is the only weapon given to you in your armor. His robe is dipped in blood because it is His blood that saved us. That is the testimony of Jesus. His name is the Word of God. Remember what John said?

John 1:1-2 In the beginning was the Word and the Word was with God, and the Word was God. He was with God in the beginning.

He has many crowns on His head. He is ruler over everything. The name on His thigh is King of Kings and Lord of Lords. He is the only one true God and He rules and reigns forever. Hallelujah! He is the picture of victory. His final entrance sums up everything: He is faithful and true, He is returning like He said He would, He is a righteous judge, He was victorious on the cross and He is the almighty ruler, the name above all names, the fulfiller of the Word of God. The weapons of your warfare are the Word of God (the Bible), the name of Jesus, His blood and the power of your testimony. Everything Jesus is dressed in when He comes back. They all involve your mouth. If you can get this in you, you will be changed. Can you see how important the Word is? The whole purpose of this book is to get you interested enough to pick up the Holy Bible and read it yourself so you will have the Word in you. Jesus has given you the victory through His blood. The Bible tells you how to live your new life in Him.

Ephesians 6 tells us how to put on our armor so that when the day of evil comes, we may be able to stand our ground. The bible says to "put on, stand firm, take up" the full armor. Not just some parts of it, but all of the armor because it works together. It requires action on our part. You put on the armor before the day of evil comes so that when it does come you are ready.

Ephesians 6:10-18 Finally, be strong in the Lord and in his mighty power. Put on the full armor of God so that you can take your stand against the devil's schemes. For our struggle is not against flesh and blood, but against the rulers, against the authorities, against the powers of this dark world and against the spiritual forces of evil in the heavenly realms. Therefore, put on the full armor of God, so that when the day of evil comes, you may be able to stand your ground, and after you have done everything, to stand. Stand firm then, with the belt of truth buckled around your waist, with the breastplate of righteousness in place, and with your feet fitted with the readiness that comes from the gospel of peace. In addition to all this, take up the shield of faith, with which you can extinguish all the flaming arrows of the evil one. Take the helmet of salvation and the sword of the Spirit, which is the word of God. And pray in the Spirit on all occasions with all kinds of prayers and requests. With this in mind, be alert and always keep on praying for all the saints.

Your strength is in the Lord and His mighty power, not your own. Your helmet is your salvation. If you don't belong to God, you belong to the enemy. How can you fight the enemies of God if you are not on His side? Once you belong to God, you have to renew your mind. You can't do that if you don't know Him. You get to know Him by reading the Bible. You are sure of your salvation and your mind is filled with God's Word. You use the Word you have stored in your heart and mind to fight the enemy with your mouth.

Jeremiah 15:16 Thy words were found, and I did eat them; and thy word was unto me the joy and rejoicing of mine heart: for I am called by thy name, O Lord God of hosts.

Romans 12:2 Do not conform any longer to the pattern of this world, but be transformed by the renewing of your mind. Then you will be able to test and approve what God's will is – His good, pleasing and perfect will.

The breastplate of righteousness protects your heart and means you are right with God. You live and move and breathe and have your being in Him. His Word is safely stored in your heart and the way you live your life reflects your salvation.

The belt of truth, the truth of the Word of God, is not dangling around your waist, it is girt, buckled, synched. It is secure around your waist. The truth holds all the other armor in place. The belt means that you live and are secure in God's truth. You speak truth and you live truthfully according to the Word.

Next, your feet are shod with the preparation of the gospel of peace. You don't go into battle unprepared. When a horse is shod, its shoes are nailed to its feet. Those babies are not coming off. You can march yourself straight into a battle because you are prepared with the gospel of Jesus and the peace is the victory of His blood. You are filled with God's peace, not mans. You are dressed in peace and wherever you walk you spread His peace. The battle belongs to the Lord, and He marches out before you.

The shield of faith is used to quench all the fiery darts of the devil. You know the truth so your faith kicks in and the things of the devil don't get inside you. They bounce off your breastplate and your shield and your helmet. They don't get in your heart and mind.

99

Finally, take the helmet of salvation and the sword of the Spirit, which is the Word of God. Nothing else works without the helmet. You cannot use the tools of God if you are not His. You believe all of God's Word or none. This is action armor. You take up, put on, stand firm, buckle your belt, fit your feet, take up the shield, take the sword, pray in the spirit, be alert and keep on praying. This is not for pew potatoes. This is warrior stuff which is translated: normal Christian living.

When you get saved by asking Jesus into your heart, the helmet of your salvation covers your head, which includes your eyes, ears, mouth and brain. These are the portals to your heart. It is how you fill your heart with God's stuff. The Bible is your sword. It is your faith in God and His Word that you have packed in your heart by way of your eyes, ears and mind that wins the battle. It is the only weapon in your suit of armor and its power is unleashed with your mouth. The spoken Word of God is your weapon in battle. When you combine the Word of God with prayer, you are swinging a lethal sword.

The sword of the Spirit is the Word of God in your mouth. The Word is activated by your mouth, which was motivated by your heart, which was fed by your mind when you got the Word in you by reading it with your eyes and hearing it with your ears. The eyes of your heart have been enlightened so you will know (there are your thoughts again) His hope, His inheritance and His power. That is our faith. That power, by the way, is the same power that raised Jesus from the dead (Ephesians 1:17-23). That is huge! The sword of the Spirit, which is the Word of God, combined with praying in the Spirit on all occasions is enough. It is the only weapon we need. PRAY WORD! That is the power of God at work in and through you. It raises the dead. It is where the supernatural takes place. It is how wars are fought and won. God's spoken word is what activated His Holy Spirit to get busy with the creation of the universe, remember? The Holy Spirit was hovering over the waters waiting for God to say "Let there be." This is why Satan wants your mind. He doesn't want you to be filled with God's Holy Spirit. He tries to get under your helmet by placing his stuff before your eyes and ears so his junk will come out of your mouth because you allowed it to get into your heart by what you fed your mind. But you take up your shield of faith and beat him down with the sword of the Spirit, hallelujah!

So the helmet, breastplate, belt, shoes and shield all have to do with what you *know* about the Word of God. (Salvation, righteousness, truth, peace, and faith) The sword is what you *do* with the Word of God. The armor is the Word inside you; what you know and believe. It strengthens you. When you read the Word out loud with your eyes and your mouth, you get the Word in your eyes and ears and it feeds your soul (mind, will and emotions). It is applied to your heart and comes out your mouth. Out of the heart the mouth speaks.

Your mouth becomes a weapon when you use it as a sword by the words that come out of it. But be careful because you can also curse yourself with your mouth and cancel your own prayers by being double minded. You become double minded when you speak what is contrary to the Word. You do that because your faith is low.

James 1:5-8 If any of you lacks wisdom, he should ask God, who gives generously to all without finding fault, and it will be given to him. But when he asks, he must believe and not doubt, because he who doubts is like a wave of the sea, blown and tossed by the wind. That man should not think he will receive anything from the Lord; he is a double-minded man, unstable in all he does.

Romans 10:8-10 But what does it say? "The word is near you; it is in your mouth and in your heart," that is, the word of faith we are proclaiming: That if you confess with your mouth, "Jesus is Lord," and believe in your heart that God raised him from the dead, you will be saved. For it is with your heart that you believe and are justified, and it is with your mouth that you confess and are saved.

Your testimony is in your mouth. That is why Satan wants to control your thoughts and set his lies before your eyes. If he can do that, he has your heart and your mind and your mouth and your confession and he is able to leave you powerless so you won't win your own battles and you cannot influence others and win them to Christ. He wants to ruin your testimony. But we shouldn't give the enemy too much credit. Many of the decisions we make are because of our own sin nature and lack of self-discipline. We can be rotten on our own without the enemies help if we don't obey the Bible.

The way you live your life is part of your testimony. If you are living contrary to how the Bible tells you to live or what you say you believe in God's Word, your testimony is no good and you become a stumbling block to the unsaved. Until repentance takes place, you cannot move on in the business of God. When people around you who are not saved see how you live, whether good or bad, they judge God and His church for it. We need to bear good fruit.

Colossians 3:8 But now you must also rid yourselves of all such things as these: anger, rage, malice, slander, and filthy language from your lips.

We can learn a lot about the power of our mouths by looking at Numbers 13 and 14. God told Moses to send men into Canaan to explore the land he was giving them. Twelve men, one from each tribe of Israel were sent in. They were to check things out and come back with a good report. God had already told them He was giving them a land flowing with milk and honey. He had been saying that ever since Abraham, but when they were in captivity in Egypt, the parents quit telling their children about God and they lost their relationship with Him. So they come out of Egypt and again God is telling them about the Promised Land. He is creating a new nation and building a new relationship with them with signs and wonders and miracles. They were at Mt.

Sinai for a year where they received the Torah and the Ten Commandments. Now a few months later they are finally going to see the Promised Land for themselves. God said to send one leader from every tribe. God must have been very excited to show them what He had for them.

Moses told them to come back with a full report, so off the twelve go and for forty days they spy out the land. Israel waits in eager anticipation for the wonderful report. Before the spies returned to Moses, they gathered grapes, figs and pomegranates to show the people that it is indeed a fertile land just as God had said. God is setting His promise before their eyes.

Numbers 13:26-33 They came back to Moses and Aaron and the whole Israelite community at Kadesh in the Desert of Paran. There they reported to them and to the whole assembly and showed them the fruit of the land. They gave Moses this account: "We went into the land to which you sent us, and it does flow with milk and honey! Here is its fruit. But the people who live there are powerful and the cities are fortified and very large. We even saw descendants of Anak there. The Amalekites live in the Negev; the Hittites, Jebusites and Amorites live in the hill country; and the Canaanites live near the sea and along the Jordan." Then Caleb silenced the people before Moses and said, "We should go up and take possession of the land, for we can certainly do it."

But the men who had gone up with him said, "We can't attack those people; they are stronger than we are." And they spread among the Israelites a bad report about the land they had explored. They said, "The land we explored devours those living in it. All the people we saw there are of great size. We saw the Nephilim there (the descendants of Anak come from the Nephilim). We seemed like grasshoppers in our own eyes, and we looked the same to them."

Ok. The whole Israelite community, the whole assembly, men, women and children have gathered to hear what the spies have to say. They are very excited. They have come out of 400 years of slavery in Egypt and they are about to go into the promised land that Abraham spoke of so long ago. The land God promised would belong to them and their offspring forever, flowing with milk and honey. They are looking forward to an awesome report of a land they will call their very own home. Forty days is a long time to wait when you are excited.

When the spies got back, they showed the people the wonderful fruit and said that it was indeed a land flowing with milk and honey, but here is why we can't do this. Then they told the people why God's long promised gift, their inheritance, was not a good land. Oh no! Can you imagine how the Israelites must have felt? The spies put fear in the hearts of the people and changed the report of what God told them. They relied on what they saw with their eyes, not any kind of faith stored in their hearts. They said there were giants in the land and the cities were large and fortified. They said, "We can't attack these people; they are stronger than we are." Wait, what? Wait a minute. That is not what God said! What did God tell them only a zillion times? Let's go back about 600 years.

Genesis 13:14-17 The Lord said to Abram after Lot had parted from him, "Lift up your eyes from where you are and look north and south, east and west. All the land that you see I will give to you and your offspring forever. I will make your offspring like the dust of the earth, so that if anyone could count the dust, then your offspring could be counted. Go; walk through the length and breadth of the land, for I am giving it to you."

Abraham lived in Canaan. He got to walk the land. God said, "I am giving it to you forever." God would do the work. It was a gift to His people.

Genesis 15:13-14 Then the Lord said to him, "Know for certain that your descendants will be strangers in a country not their own, and they will be enslaved and mistreated four hundred years. But I will punish the nation they serve as slaves, and afterward they will come out with great possessions.

That's you Israel! Don't you remember what God told your father Abraham? It was a covenant promise between God and the descendants of Abraham.

Genesis 15:18-21 On that day the Lord made a covenant with Abram and said, "To your descendants I give this land, from the river of Egypt to the great river, the Euphrates – the land of the Kenites, Kenizzites, Kadmonites, Hittites, Perizzites, Girgashites and Jebusites."

Don't you remember what Moses told you God said?

Exodus 34:11 Obey what I command you today. I will drive out before you the Amorites, Canaanites, Hittites, Perizzites, Hivites and Jebusites.

You left Egypt for this very day to come to this very place. God told you He would be the one to drive out your enemies. God will give them into your hands. God will give you the land. Why did the explorers come back and say "We can't do it" when God is the one doing it? Let's look at what God told Moses just forty days before.

Numbers 13:1-2 the Lord said to Moses, "Send some men to explore the land of Canaan, which I am giving to the Israelites. From each ancestral tribe send one of its leaders."

These twelve men were leaders of the tribes. God said, "I am giving to the Israelites." God has never lied to them. As leaders their faith in what God said should have been set. They were in Canaan for forty days and nobody in the land devoured them. Their eyes trumped their faith and the yeast infection of the exaggerated words of their mouths filled the camp of Israel. Their faithless report influenced the people who did not see the land to say something absolutely horrific.

Numbers 14:1-4 That night all the people of the community raised their voices and wept aloud. All the Israelites grumbled against Moses and Aaron, and the whole assembly said to them, "If only we had died in Egypt! Or in this desert! Why is the Lord bringing us to this land only to let us fall by the sword? Our wives and children will be taken as plunder. Wouldn't it be better for us to go back to Egypt?" And they said to each other, "We should choose a leader and go back to Egypt."

Oh Israel, you did not just say that. Fear and unbelief caused them to reject the gift of God that was promised for so long. They forgot the persecution in Egypt. They forgot how long it took Moses to get them out of there. They forgot about the sea parting for them and that their water came from the rock and their food from God Himself. Now they want to die in Egypt. They cry out loud and grumble. They accuse God of trying to kill them in the desert and call Egypt better. They accuse God of not protecting their wives and children, and as a final insult, they verbally reject God as their leader by saying they should choose another and go back into captivity. They don't fear God; they fear Canaan. It should have been the other way around. That is what weak faith does. That is exactly what happens when your eyes and ears believe what they see and hear. It's because you don't have anything stored in your heart. It is the stronghold of the enemy the Bible warns us about.

Job 12:11 Does not the ear test words as the tongue tastes food?

That is what happens when we don't have a relationship with God. We don't spend time with God and get to know how great He is and we don't store His words in our hearts to build our faith in our minds. We don't talk to God in prayer. The relationship Israel wanted was visible proof. They had that already. What they lacked was a relationship built on faith. They said they would rather die in the desert and that is what they got. Now they will spend forty years wandering in the desert until the last of them who complained die because of what came out of their mouths. One year for each day the spies were in the promised land.

Proverbs 4:24 Keep your mouth free of perversity; keep corrupt talk far from your lips.

Proverbs 18:21 The tongue has the power of life and death, and those who love it will eat its fruit.

Proverbs 30:32 If you have played the fool and exalted yourself, or if you have planned evil, clap your hand over your mouth!

Matthew 15:18 But the things that come out of a person's mouth come from the heart, and these defile them.

James 1:26 If anyone considers himself religious and yet does not keep a tight rein on his tongue, he deceives himself and his religion is worthless.

Your words are very powerful. They have the power to build up or tear down. Instead of building the faith of the people with the promises of God, the spies allowed the enemy of God to put his stuff before their eyes and his lies in their ears so theirs hearts were filled with fear. They called God a liar in front of the men, women and children of Israel. If the leaders are afraid, it must be bad. The shock of the report and what the people were saying was so terrible against God, Moses and Aaron literally fell to the ground. It was Joshua and Caleb who spoke.

Numbers 14:5-9 Then Moses and Aaron fell face down in front of the whole Israelite assembly gathered there. Joshua, son of Nun and Caleb, son of Jephunneh, who were among those who had explored the land, tore their clothes and said to the entire Israelite assembly, "The land we passed through and explored is exceedingly good. If the Lord is pleased with us, he will lead us into that land, a land flowing with milk and honey, and will give it to us. Only do not rebel against the Lord. And do not be afraid of the people of the land, because we will swallow them up. Their protection is gone, but the Lord is with us. Do not be afraid of them."

Ten saw giants, two saw grapes. The evil, unbelieving words of ten men drowned out the hope of the promise spoken by the two. The bad report of just ten men influenced more than a million people. Wasn't there anyone else who believed out of all those present that day who would speak out for God and His wonderful promise? The Bible tells us that "all" the community grumbled. Only Joshua and Caleb came back with a good report.

1 Peter 3:10 For, "Whoever would love life and see good days must keep his tongue from evil and his lips from deceitful speech."

Proverbs 14:5 A truthful witness does not deceive, but a false witness pours out lies.

Caleb tried to silence Israel and encourage them with God's promises. That night Joshua and Caleb tried one more time to rally the people. They spoke out in great faith, but the damage of the bad report was too much. Now the people want to stone them. First of all, you don't touch God's anointed. Second, what came out of their mouths was so blasphemous it sent Moses and Aaron to the ground. Now it is night. God has not spoken yet and neither has Moses or Aaron. They are filled with the fear of the Lord. That is an awesome thing. It is proof of a relationship with God Almighty as your Abba Father, Daddy. The Bible tells us that the fear of the Lord brings wisdom. Oh, if only Israel had that same relationship. If they had been filled with God stuff in their hearts, they would have picked up stones and silenced the ten. They would have been on their faces along with Moses and Aaron, and they would have received the blessings of God. But they are not on their faces and now they stand with their children before a very angry God who is not only ready to speak but He appears to them in His Glory. God speaks to Moses only at first.

Numbers 14:10-12 But the whole assembly talked about stoning them. Then the glory of the Lord appeared at the Tent of Meeting to all the Israelites. The Lord said to Moses, "How long will these people treat me with contempt? How long will they refuse to believe in me, in spite of all the miraculous signs I have performed among them? I will strike them down with a plague and destroy them, but I will make you into a nation greater and stronger than they."

The eyes, ears, mouth, heart and mind of Moses completely belong to God, and he intercedes for the people because of God's name. Learn from this church! How much do you love God's name? How much love is there in your heart for an evil people?

Numbers 14:13-19 Moses said to the Lord, "Then the Egyptians will hear about it! By your power you brought these people up from among them. And they will tell the inhabitants of this land about it. They have already heard that you, O Lord, are with these people and that you, O Lord, have been seen face to face, that your cloud stays over them, and that you go before them in a pillar of cloud by day and a pillar of fire by night. If you put these people to death all at one time, the nations who have heard this report about you will say, 'The Lord was not able to bring these people into the land he promised them on oath; so he slaughtered them in the desert.' Now may the Lord's strength be displayed, just as you have declared: 'The Lord is slow to anger, abounding in love and forgiving sin and rebellion. Yet he does not leave the guilty unpunished; he punishes the children for the sin of the fathers to the third and fourth generation.' In accordance with your great love, forgive the sin of these people, just as you have pardoned them from the time they left Egypt until now."

Moses was concerned about the reputation of God. He was concerned about the people he was responsible for. He reminds God of His Word and His great love and forgiveness. If you compare the prayer of Moses to the prayer Jesus prayed in Gethsemane, you will see the same mind and heart condition. Two hearts completely filled with God's love praying for the salvation of an unholy people.

109

John 17:20-23 "My prayer is not for them alone. I pray also for those who will believe in me through their message, that all of them may be one, Father, just as you are in me and I am in you. May they also be in us so that the world may believe that you have sent me. I have given them the glory that you gave me, that they may be one as we are one: I in them and you in me. May they be brought to complete unity to let the world know that you sent me and have loved them even as you have loved me."

You don't get that kind of heart by ignoring God. You don't come into that kind of wisdom by ignoring the Word of God. You cannot form a relationship with your Creator by living according to the standards of the world. What do you want? Who do you love?

Romans 8:5-8 Those who live according to the sinful nature have their minds set on what that nature desires; but those who live in accordance with the Spirit have their minds set on what the Spirit desires. The mind of sinful man is death, but the mind controlled by the Spirit is life and peace; the sinful mind is hostile to God. It does not submit to God's law, nor can it do so. Those controlled by the sinful nature cannot please God.

God honored the prayer of Moses and forgave the people, but the punishment was severe. If Moses had not interceded for the people, God would have wiped them out then and there He was so mad. The reason God gets so mad is because after all He has done for us, we still don't trust Him. Where is our faith? Are we any different than the Israelites?

Hebrews 11:6 And without faith it is impossible to please God, because anyone who comes to him must believe that he exists and that he rewards those who earnestly seek him.

Micah 6:8 He has showed you, O man, what is good. And what does the Lord require of you: To act justly and to love mercy and to walk humbly with your God.

When we walk with God, He gives us life and life abundantly. We listen to the enemy instead to get what we want. But the prayers of a righteous man avail much (James 5:16) and Moses is on it. He interceded for the people and God answered.

Numbers 14:20-25 The Lord replied, "I have forgiven them, as you asked. Nevertheless, as surely as I live and as surely as the glory of the Lord fills the whole earth, not one of the men who saw my glory and the miraculous signs I performed in Egypt and in the desert but who disobeyed me and tested me ten times — not one of them will ever see the land I promised on oath to their forefathers. No one who has treated me with contempt will ever see it. But because my servant Caleb has a different spirit and follows me wholeheartedly, I will bring him into the land he went to, and his descendants will inherit it. Since the Amalekites and Canaanites are living in the valleys, turn back tomorrow and set out toward the desert along the route to the Red Sea."

The Israelites were right there! They were right there at the door of their promise, but the words of their mouths cancelled the wonderful gift of God for them, and it was given to their children instead. Now they can't go in. They have to go back into the desert and wander until they die. How depressed would you be? Do you remember as a child you wanted to do something fun but you disobeyed and your father wouldn't let you? That was just for a day. This punishment was for life. That is how important the words are that come out of your mouth towards God. That is how you test your heart.

Psalm 19:14 May the words of my mouth and the meditations of my heart be pleasing in your sight, O Lord, my Rock and my Redeemer.

Can you imagine how they must have felt? You cannot take back the words of your mouth. When they are out, they are out.

Numbers 14:26-38 The Lord said to Moses and Aaron: "How long will this wicked community grumble against me? I have heard the complaints of these grumbling Israelites. So tell them, 'As surely as I live, declares the Lord, <u>I will do to you the very things I heard you say</u>: In this desert your bodies will fall—every one of you twenty years old or more who was counted in the census and who has grumbled against me. Not one of you will enter the land I swore with uplifted hand to make your home, except Caleb son of Jephunneh and Joshua son of Nun. As for your children that you said would be taken as plunder, I will bring them in to enjoy the land you have rejected. But you—your bodies will fall in this desert. Your children will be shepherds here for forty years, suffering for your unfaithfulness, until the last of your bodies lies in the desert. For forty years—one year for each of the forty days you explored the land—you will suffer for your sins and know what it is like to have me against you.' I, the Lord, have spoken, and I will surely do these things to this whole wicked community, which has banded together against me. They will meet their end in this desert; here they will die."

So the men Moses had sent to explore the land, who returned and made the whole community grumble against him by spreading a bad report about it— these men responsible for spreading the bad report about the land were struck down and died of a plague before the Lord. Of the men who went to explore the land, only Joshua son of Nun and Caleb son of Jephunneh survived.

The words of Joshua and Caleb saved them. Their spoken out loud faith in God allowed them to receive the promise of their inheritance. It would be delayed 40 years but they were going in.

Proverbs 14:3 A fool's talk brings a rod to his back, but the lips of the wise protect them.

Now God has spoken. His words are final and what He decreed was done, that's it. The ten men were killed then and

112

there before the people. Moses told the people what God said and the Bible says they mourned bitterly. What a lesson for us all. Israel tried to fix it themselves by moving ahead anyway without God and that didn't work either.

Numbers 14:39-45 When Moses reported this to all the Israelites, they mourned bitterly. Early the next morning they went up toward the high hill country. "We will go up to the place the Lord promised." But Moses said, "Why are you disobeying the Lord's command? This will not succeed! Do not go up, because the Lord is not with you. You will be defeated by your enemies. For the Amalekites and Canaanites will face you there. Because you have turned away from the Lord, he will not be with you and you will fall by the sword. Nevertheless, in their presumption they went up toward the High hill country, though neither Moses nor the ark of the Lord's covenant moved from the camp. Then the Amalekites and Canaanites who lived in that hill country came down attacked them and beat them down all the way to Hormah.

Do you see the heart condition here? They feel bad and they want to fix things but not because they want to obey God. They want their own way. You can tell because they are still disobeying. Moses said don't go, you will not succeed, because God will not be with you and off they went. They went without God, Moses, the cloud and the Ark and got beat up for it.

Now they have to wander in the desert for forty years until the disobedient generation died. Only their children would receive the promise. They would spend this time building a relationship with God as their Father who loved them.

Proverbs 15:2 The tongue of the wise commends knowledge, but the mouth of the fool gushes folly.

James 3:6 The tongue also is a fire, a world of evil among the parts of the body. It corrupts the whole person, sets the whole course of his life on fire, and is itself set on fire by hell.

James 3:9-10 With the tongue we praise our Lord and Father, and with it we curse men, who have been made in God's likeness. Out of the same mouth come praise and cursing. My brothers, this should not be.

Now let's cheer up and look at a King who knew God and the words of his mouth brought victory instead of rebuke.

Asa was one of the few good kings. The Bible tells us that Asa did what was good and right in the eyes of the Lord his God. God was Asa's Lord. Like Abraham before him, Asa commanded Judah to seek the Lord the God of their fathers, and to obey His laws and commands. Did you get that? Asa commanded the people. Again they have to be commanded to do it just in case they wouldn't do it on their own and just like Abraham it worked. Asa got rid of all of the idols and all the junk that went with them. Because of his obedience, God gave him rest and Judah prospered. Asa told the people that the land was still theirs because they sought the Lord. The reward for their obedience was peace. Pay attention to that. The reward for our obedience is peace and that is a sweet reward. If you have ever been in turmoil or deep distress, you understand what a huge gift peace is. When you are at peace, you are free to focus on other things. Asa told the people that since they obeyed God and were now at peace, they could build and fortify their towns. So they built and prospered (2 Chronicles 14:7). Don't you love that? They not only had peace, but they built and prospered too. God is so rich towards us. It went on for years it says.

So Asa and the people live in peace and fortify their towns. Then here come Zerah the Cushite with a gargantuan army to mess it all up. Do you see? Satan brings out the spirit of fear and sets it before Asa's' eyes. If Satan can get the leader to fall, the whole kingdom will fall with him. But Asa is ready for him. He and his people have been walking with God for years, so their faith is strong and their eyes are set like flint and there is no fear in them, hallelujah! Asa is not focused on the size of the armies. Instead of cowering behind his newly built walls, he marches his troops out to meet Zerah and takes up his battle position. His army is not murmuring or complaining.

When you keep your eyes in God's Word and walk with God continuously and it is a lifestyle you live in day-to-day and not just a sometimes thing, you are ready for everything that comes along without fainting. You are always ready for the Master's use. The key is to decide which master you are going to be ready for. God is Asa's Master. Asa marches Judah out to meet Zerah and they did something spectacular. You have to read it!

2 Chronicles 14:9-11 Zerah the Cushite marched out against them with a vast army and three hundred chariots, and came as far as Mareshah. Asa went out to meet him, and they took up battle positions in the Valley of Zephathah near Mareshah. Then Asa called to the Lord his God and said, "Lord, there is no one like you to help the powerless against the mighty. Help us, O Lord our God, for we rely on you, and in your name we have come against this vast army. O Lord, you are our God; do not let man prevail against you."

You talk about faith. This is it! Can you picture it? It was a David and Goliath moment. There was silence all around. Two armies are facing each other waiting to hear the trumpet blast to move forward. Satan has put his stuff before the eyes of God's army. A vast army is coming at them. Vast means really, really enormous! Not only that but they have three hundred chariots. If it is you on foot against a chariot, the chariot will win. That is unless God is on your side. Remember, God won't let His armies have lots of stuff to fight with because God goes before them. God is their Deliverer. Asa's army has shields, spears and bows. The chariots would be idols to Israel because they would put more trust in them than they would in God. The battle belongs to the Lord. Asa is putting his faith in action.

It would have been terrifying to see if Asa and Judah had been looking with human eyes. But Asa was using his spiritual eyes. The faith that was stored in his heart and mind came out of his mouth and strengthened his army. Greater was He that was in Asa than he that was in the valley. Before fear has a chance to set in, before the signal sounds, one lone voice cried out to God so that all could hear. That voice reverberated off the hills and pierced the hearts of everyone who heard it. It strengthened one army and terrified the other! "IT IS ALL ABOUT YOU LORD. WE ARE POWERLESS BUT YOU ARE GOD AND THERE IS NO ONE LIKE YOU. YOU ARE OUR ONLY HOPE AND IN YOUR NAME WE ARE GOING TO FIGHT THIS BATTLE. DON'T LET MAN RUIN YOUR NAME." Did you hear that? That is the same thing Moses said! That is the same heart for God. It only takes one voice to influence the many. The next verse:

2 Chronicles 14:12-13 The Lord struck down the Cushites before Asa and Judah. The Cushites fled and Asa and his army pursued them as far as Gerar.

That's the joy of the Lord! The Bible says in verse 13 that the Cushites were crushed before the Lord and His forces. The Cushites were defeated and Judah got to keep the Cushites stuff. Judah got the peace and the plunder. The Bible says that the terror of the Lord had fallen upon all the villages around Gerar. They weren't afraid of Asa, they were afraid of his God! Zerah saw how small Judah's army was and God's miracle was a no-brainer. It was obviously the God of Judah who brought about the Cushite defeat.

God promises us in His Word that if we will trust in Him, He will deliver us. God loves it when we trust Him so He can make His glory known among us. Memorize 2 Chronicles 14:11 and personalize it.

"Lord, there is no one like you to help me against the mighty. Help me O Lord my God, for I rely on you, and in your name I have come against this _____. O Lord, you are my God; do not let man prevail against you."

That is how you use the sword of the Spirit, which is the Word of God (Ephesians 6:17). You speak God's Words out loud in faith. The more you hang out with God in His Word, the more you trust Him and the bigger your faith grows. The Holy Spirit in you rises above your flesh. Your testimony grows and others see what is happening in your life and God gets the glory. That is what happened to the people in Israel when they saw that God was with Judah. Large numbers moved to Judah. Your spirit wants to be where God is.

But there is more. After a victory, you have some spiritual housework to do. The victory is wonderful, but don't forget how you got there. It is very easy to get caught up in the victory and quit watching what is going on around you. After a victory is not the time to take a spiritual break.

2 Chronicles 15:1-2 The Spirit of God came upon Azariah son of Oded. He went out to meet Asa and said to him, "Listen to me, Asa and all Judah and Benjamin. The Lord is with you when you are with him. If you seek him, he will be found by you, but if you forsake him, he will forsake you."

2 Chronicles 15:7 But as for you, be strong and do not give up, for your work will be rewarded.

Forsake also means abandon or withdraw. Don't forget God. Now it had been a while since the war with the Cushites and Asa had some work to do so the enemy wouldn't get a foothold in Judah. Already the idols were back. When Asa heard the words of Azariah, he took courage and got busy. He needed courage for the huge job he had to do. He had to remove the idols from the towns he captured and he had to clean up Judah again. He wasn't watching and the idols sneaked their way back into Judah with the masses of people who moved there. He repaired the altar of the Lord and assembled all the people. He had to get all the people together again so that there would be unity and the newcomers would enter into the covenant with Judah. If they

117

were going to live in Judah, they had to follow God so they sacrificed to the Lord and entered into a covenant as one people.

2 Chronicles 15:12-15 They entered into a covenant to seek the Lord, the God of their fathers, with all their heart and soul. All who would not seek the Lord, the God of Israel, were to be put to death, whether small or great, man or woman. They took an oath to the Lord with loud acclamation, with shouting and with trumpets and horns. All Judah rejoiced about the oath because they had sworn it wholeheartedly. They sought God eagerly, and he was found by them. So the Lord gave them rest on every side.

Remember, the people who moved to Judah were from other tribes of Israel. They were in the covenant law given to Moses by God at Mt. Sinai but they had become idolaters. Now they have made a new covenant *(with loud acclamation, with shouting and with trumpets and horns)* to follow God wholeheartedly and there was no more war for a long time because God gave them rest.

It is when you are at peace that you get lazy if you are not careful. The victory over the Cushite army by God years earlier was a dull memory at best and now the army of Israel is coming up against Judah. This time instead of calling out to God for help, Asa buys his victory from a foreign, ungodly King. Why did he do that?

2 Chronicles 16:7-9 At that time Hanani the seer came to Asa king of Judah and said to him: "Because you relied on the king of Aram and not on the Lord your God, the army of the king of Aram has escaped from your hand. Were not the Cushites and Libyans a mighty army with great numbers of chariots and horsemen? Yet when you relied on the Lord, he delivered them into your hand. <u>For the eyes of the Lord range throughout the earth to strengthen those whose hearts are fully committed to him.</u> You have done a foolish thing and from now on you will be at war."

Do you understand? It may look like Asa won a victory on the surface but because he did it in his own way he left all kinds of loose ends. When God takes over for you His deliverance is perfect. There is nothing left undone. Now Judah is left with an alliance with a foreign king who should have been defeated. This means years of consequences.

The fact that Asa didn't call on God tells us that his relationship with God had changed. He took what he thought was the easy road. He didn't get that check in his spirit that says to ask God first because he didn't recognize the voice of God anymore. Remember the rules for the king given in Deuteronomy? If you are reading your Bible every day, you don't forget God's voice. God's Holy Spirit will remind you of what you read in the Bible when you need it. He can't bring back to you what you have not read with your eyes. When you read the Bible, you learn to revere God. Revere means to respect and worship.

Deuteronomy 17:18-19 When he takes the throne of his kingdom, he is to write for himself on a scroll a copy of this law, taken from that of the priests, who are Levites. It is to be with him, and he is to read it all the days of his life so that he may learn to revere the Lord his God and follow carefully all the words of this law and these decrees...

Somewhere along the line, Asa quit reading the law. He quit spending time with his God so when he needed help, the first thing that came to mind was not to call on God, but to make a treaty with a foreign king because that seemed easier. Hanani the seer came to see Asa and called him on the carpet for it. He gave Asa the message from God that from now on he would be at war. There would be no more peace.

Do you remember what David said when Nathan confronted him about his sin with Bathsheba? He said simply, "I have sinned against the Lord." It was instant repentance. Not so with Asa. When Hanani confronted Asa about not calling on God, Asa was so enraged that he put Hanani in prison. That wasn't enough to make him feel better so he also brutally oppressed some of the people. Good heavens!!! A simple "I'm sorry" would have dramatically changed everything. Why did he get so mad?

When you move away from God, you become fleshy. Your reactions to difficult situations become worldly instead of Godly. You become reactive instead of proactive. Self-pity and your desire to pay back instead of drawing near becomes the god of choice. The pressure is on because you are relying on your own efforts instead of asking God for help. Asa was afflicted with a disease in his feet and still he did not call on the Lord for his healing. He died in that spiritual and physical condition. It didn't have to be like that.

2 Chronicles 16:12-13 In the thirty-ninth year of his reign Asa was afflicted with a disease in his feet. Though his disease was severe, even in his illness he did not seek help from the Lord, but only from the physicians. Then in the forty-first year of his reign Asa died and rested with his fathers.

The eyes of the Lord still range throughout the earth to strengthen those whose hearts are fully committed to Him.

1 Peter 3:10-12 For, "Whoever would love life and see good days must keep his tongue from evil and his lips from deceitful speech. He must turn from evil and do good; he must seek peace and pursue it. For the eyes of the Lord are on the righteous and his ears are attentive to their prayer, but the face of the Lord is against those who do evil."

Proverbs 12:18 Reckless words pierce like a sword, but the tongue of the wise brings healing.

Proverbs 11:13 A gossip betrays a confidence, but a trustworthy man keeps a secret.

Proverbs 16:28 A perverse man stirs up dissension, and a gossip separates close friends.

1 Timothy 5:13-14 Besides, they get into the habit of being idle and going about from house to house. And not only do they become idlers, but also gossips and busybodies, saying things they ought not to. So I counsel younger widows to marry, to have children, to manage their homes and to give the enemy no opportunity for slander.

It is so hard to watch what we say. God hates gossip. We blurt out things we wish we hadn't said because of the emotion of the moment. If we could just learn to wait a few seconds before we speak out we would be so glad we didn't say it. If we would learn to speak victory like Asa instead of defeat, God could use us more. There would be more victory in our everyday lives and we would sow a better testimony. What comes out of your mouth tells the world and God what is in your heart. By our words we will be acquitted, and by our words we will be condemned (Matthew 12: 37).

James 3:9-18 With the tongue we praise our Lord and Father, and with it we curse men, who have been made in God's likeness. Out of the same mouth come praise and cursing. My brothers, this should not be. Can both fresh water and saltwater flow from the same spring? My brothers, can a fig tree bear olives, or a grapevine bear figs? Neither can a salt spring produce fresh water. Who is wise and understanding among you? Let him show it by his good life, by deeds done in the humility that comes from wisdom. But if you harbor bitter envy and selfish ambition in your hearts, do not boast about it or deny the truth. Such "wisdom" does not come down from heaven but is earthly, unspiritual, of the devil. For where you have envy and selfish ambition, there you find disorder and every evil practice. But the wisdom that comes from heaven is first of all pure; then peace-loving, considerate, submissive, full of mercy and good fruit, impartial and sincere. Peacemakers who sow in peace raise a harvest of righteousness.

Psalm 119:171-173 May my lips overflow with praise, for you teach me your decrees. May my tongue sing of your word, for all your commands are righteous. May your hand be ready to help me, for I have chosen your precepts.

Matthew 12:35-37 The good man brings good things out of the good stored up in him, and the evil man brings evil things out of the evil stored up in him. But I tell you that men will have to give account on the day of judgment for every careless word they have spoken. For by your words you will be acquitted, and by your words you will be condemned.

Chapter 6
THE ARMY AND THE ENEMY

Ephesians 6:10-12
Finally, be strong in the Lord and in His mighty power. Put on the full
armor of God so that you can take your stand against the devil's schemes.
For our struggle is not against flesh and blood, but against the rulers,
against the authorities, against the powers of this dark world and against
the spiritual forces of evil in the heavenly realms.

God's army is precious to Him. We are His children. He is our Father, Protector, Provider, and lover of our souls. He protects us from the enemy. He taught us in His Word how to recognize, fight and win battles against the enemy. God is violent towards the enemy because the enemy is set on the destruction of us. This is a spiritual battle. The enemy knows what you know and what you don't know. Don't be afraid of the enemy; be afraid of what you don't know. Then go to the Word of God and get wisdom.

2 Corinthians 10:3-5 For though we live in the world, we do not
wage war as the world does. The weapons we fight with are not the
weapons of the world. On the contrary, they have divine power to

demolish strongholds. We demolish arguments and every pretension that sets itself up against the knowledge of God, and we take captive every thought to make it obedient to Christ.

The enemy is not people. If it were we would use worldly weapons to do battle. The world does not have strong enough weapons to destroy the enemy of God. For that, we have to use weapons with divine power. Our battle is in the heavens. Ephesians 6 tells us to take our stand against the devils schemes. Then it tells us exactly where all the trouble on the whole earth comes from.

Ephesians 6:12 For our struggle is not against flesh and blood, but against the rulers, against the authorities, against the powers of this dark world and against the spiritual forces of evil in the heavenly realms.

Our struggle is not against people, but against evil. Think about someone you don't like. Now separate the person from the problem and take a closer look. You can love the person and yet hate the sin. That's what God does. He loves us in spite of our sin because He can see what we look like without it. God offers us a way out. The key, of course, for a Christian is not to get into sin in the first place, and we have complete control over that because of the Holy Spirit in us.

Satan cannot force us to do anything. He just offers the opportunities and we take them or not. Then he sits back and watches us fall. He is a schemer. When we start to climb out of the problem, he simply sets one more opportunity in front of us and we take it and fall again and the pattern goes on until others begin to fall with us. Pretty soon we can't find God and blame the whole thing on Him for not being there for us. When you are walking with God, you recognize the source of the opportunity and you don't take it.

What is the enemy's tool of choice; our eyes. He loves to set things before our eyes that will remove our hearts and minds from our loving Creator so that we will fail; someone or something to love and worship in place of God. Satan wants to be worshiped. He tried to get Jesus to do it. He does it because he knows that God hates it. God hates it because He knows they are lies from the enemy to keep us out of heaven. Satan puts things in front of our eyes to distract us and keep our eyes off of God. He wants our thoughts. If he can plant his evil seeds in our minds, they will sprout and spread like yeast. The Bible calls them "bitter roots."

Hebrews 12:14-16 Make every effort to live in peace with all men and to be holy; without holiness no one will see the Lord. See to it that no one misses the grace of God and that no bitter root grows up to cause trouble and defile many. See that no one is sexually immoral, or is godless like Esau, who for a single meal sold his inheritance rights as the oldest son.

We need to understand that we can lose our salvation because we are without holiness. We can abuse the Grace of God because of the bitter roots in our lives that cause trouble and defile us.

The things Satan puts in front of our eyes to distract us become idols when they take the place of God and damage our testimonies. A damaged testimony is confirmation to the unsaved world that they are right. What are you hiding? It can be an actual idol of a false god, a person, addictions, an ungodly lifestyle or any sin that has control over us that removes us from the presence of God. The goal of the enemy is always the same: to keep us out of heaven. Then he wants to use us to keep others out, too. It's a satanic network marketing, so to speak, and it works like a charm.

Ezekiel 14:6-8 "Therefore say to the house of Israel, 'this is what the Sovereign Lord says: Repent! Turn from your idols and renounce all your detestable practices! When any Israelite or any alien living in Israel separates himself from me and sets up idols in his heart and puts a wicked stumbling block before his face and then goes to a prophet to inquire of me, I the Lord will answer him myself. I will set my face against that man and make him an example and a byword. I will cut him off from my people. Then you will know that I am the Lord.'"

God did not hide anything from us regarding idols. He tells us over and over that they separate us from Him and to have nothing to do with them. They are a wicked stumbling block in your face and an idol in your heart. A "block" is a good word to describe the stumbling tool of the enemy. A block where you go will trip you and make you fall away from the Lord. A block in front of your eyes will blind you and keep you from seeing the truth. A block in your ears will keep you from hearing the truth. A block in your thoughts will keep you from wisdom and understanding and a block in your heart will separate you from God. This is so easy. Satan didn't put the block in you; you did. Satan put his stuff in the world, but it didn't block you until you picked it up. Where did you go? What did you smoke? What did you drink? What did you read? Who were you with? What did you see? What did you listen to? What did you watch? What did you do? What did you say? What did you allow yourself to get into that separated you from the presence of God in your life?

Look at this verse again and realize that God is not getting mad at the devil. He doesn't mention Satan. The enemy and his stuff is not the problem. The problem is the Christian and what he does with the enemy's stuff. Israel, you, me, the church; we knowingly set up idols in our hearts. We put the stumbling blocks in front of our own faces, and when our idols don't help us and we get in trouble, we go to the Lord. Instead of repenting we say, "What's going on Lord?"

Ezekiel 14:1-6 Some of the elders of Israel came to me and sat down in front of me. Then the word of the Lord came to me: "Son of man, these men have set up idols in their hearts and put wicked stumbling blocks before their faces. Should I let them inquire of me at all? Therefore speak to them and tell them, 'This is what the Sovereign Lord says: When any

Israelite sets up idols in his heart and puts a wicked stumbling block before his face and then goes to a prophet, I the Lord will answer him myself in keeping with his great idolatry. I will do this to recapture the hearts of the people of Israel, who have all deserted me for their idols.' Therefore say to the house of Israel, 'This is what the Sovereign Lord says: Repent! Turn from your idols and renounce all your detestable practices!'"

Ezekiel was not talking to a people who did not know God. He was talking to Israel; a people who had a personal relationship with their Living God. To make matters worse, it was not just the people but the elders; the leaders. They would willingly get involved in idol worship and yet go to God with their questions. That doesn't even make sense. We are children of the Living God, descendants of Abraham and we are in the very same boat. We have set up idols of drug and alcohol abuse, sexual immorality, pornography, witchcraft, discord, etc., and when our lives are a mess and we need help, we inquire of God.

Galatians 5:16-25 So I say, live by the Spirit, and you will not gratify the desires of the sinful nature. For the sinful nature desires what is contrary to the Spirit and the Spirit what is contrary to the sinful nature. They are in conflict with each other, so that you do not do what you want. But if you are led by the Spirit, you are not under law. The acts of the sinful nature are obvious: sexual immorality, impurity and debauchery; idolatry and witchcraft; hatred, discord, jealousy, fits of rage, selfish ambition, dissensions, factions and envy; drunkenness, orgies, and the like. I warn you, as I did before, that those who live like this will not inherit the kingdom of God. But the fruit of the Spirit is love, joy, peace, patience, kindness, goodness, faithfulness, gentleness and self-control. Against such things there is no law. Those who belong to Christ Jesus have crucified the sinful nature with its passions and desires. Since we live by the Spirit, let us keep in step with the Spirit.

You can't live that way and inherit the kingdom of God. Paul is talking to the Christian church. If you die in that condition, you will not go to heaven. Adam and Eve believed in God and they got themselves kicked out of His presence because of their sin. The fallen angels believed in God and they got kicked out of His presence because of their sin. God cannot live in the presence of unrepentant sin.

Psalm 24:3-6 Who may ascend the hill of the Lord? Who may stand in his holy place? He who has clean hands and a pure heart, who does not lift up his soul to an idol or swear by what is false. He will receive blessings from the Lord and vindication from God his Savior. Such is the generation of those who seek Him, who seek your face, O God of Jacob.

Your life has to change so Jesus can recognize you when He comes back for His church. But how do we live by the Spirit? How do we fix this mess we have gotten ourselves into? How do we identify the idols in our lives? How do we know for sure that we have not set up idols? Is it too late? Does God hate us now? What do we do? This is exactly why the Bible is called "Good News."

Ephesians 4:25–5:21 Therefore each of you must put off falsehood and speak truthfully to his neighbor, for we are all members of one body. "In your anger do not sin": Do not let the sun go down while you are still angry, and do not give the devil a foothold. He who has been stealing must steal no longer, but must work, doing something useful with his own hands, that he may have something to share with those in need.

Do not let any unwholesome talk come out of your mouths, but only what is helpful for building others up according to their needs, that it may benefit those who listen. And do not grieve the Holy Spirit of God, with whom you were sealed for the day of redemption. Get rid of all bitterness, rage and anger, brawling and slander, along with every form of malice. Be kind and compassionate to one another, forgiving each other, just as in Christ God forgave you.

Be imitators of God, therefore, as dearly loved children and live a life of love, just as Christ loved us and gave himself up for us as a fragrant offering and sacrifice to God.

But among you there must not be even a hint of sexual immorality, or of any kind of impurity, or of greed, because these are improper for God's holy people. Nor should there be obscenity, foolish talk or coarse joking, which are out of place, but rather thanksgiving. For of this you can be sure: No immoral, impure or greedy person—such a man is an idolater—has any inheritance in the kingdom of Christ and of God. Let no one deceive you with empty words, for because of such things God's wrath comes on those who are disobedient. Therefore do not be partners with them.

For you were once darkness, but now you are light in the Lord. Live as children of light (for the fruit of the light consists in all goodness, righteousness and truth) and find out what pleases the Lord. Have nothing to do with the fruitless deeds of darkness, but rather expose them. For it is shameful even to mention what the disobedient do in secret. But everything exposed by the light becomes visible, for it is light that makes everything visible. This is why it is said: "Wake up, O sleeper, rise from the dead, and Christ will shine on you."

Be very careful, then, how you live—not as unwise but as wise, making the most of every opportunity, because the days are evil. Therefore do not be foolish, but understand what the Lord's will is. Do not get drunk on wine, which leads to debauchery. Instead, be filled with the Spirit. Speak to one another with psalms, hymns and spiritual songs. Sing and make music in your heart to the Lord, always giving thanks to God the Father for everything, in the name of our Lord Jesus Christ.

Submit to one another out of reverence for Christ.

That's how. It is a choice to imitate God. It is a choice to recognize that what you are doing is sin and it grieves the Holy Spirit. It is a choice to separate yourself from the sin in your life. It is a choice to watch what comes out of your mouth. You choose to be children of light or darkness. You choose to forgive. You choose to live in love and imitate God. That's how you make your life a sacrifice to God.

It is your love for God that determines your choice, and it is God's love for you that chose to forgive you no matter what when you come back to Him in repentance. How can you be sure you are living right: Because in this world, you chose to be like Him.

1 John 4:17 In this way, love is made complete among us so that we will have confidence on the day of judgment, because in this world we are like Him.

Ephesians 5:1-2 Be imitators of God, therefore, as dearly loved children and live a life of love, just as Christ loved us and gave himself up for us as a fragrant offering and sacrifice to God.

Ephesians 5:10 and find out what pleases the Lord.

But how do we imitate God? It is possible because the Bible says to do it. You do it by finding out what pleases the Lord. You ask Him. You find out by reading His Word. You earnestly seek Him. When you live your life in love like Jesus loved us and died for us, your life is a fragrant offering and a sacrifice to God (Ephesians 5:2).

Jeremiah 6:16 This is what the Lord says: "Stand at the crossroads and look; ask for the ancient paths, ask where the good way is, and walk in it, and you will find rest for your souls. But you said, 'We will not walk in it.'"

Hebrews 11:6 And without faith it is impossible to please God, because anyone who comes to him must believe that he exists and that he rewards those who earnestly seek him.

Our faith in Him is what pleases God. When you say no to sin and trust God instead, it moves the hand of God. We are not alone. Jesus promised us the Holy Spirit: one called alongside to help.

John 14:15-18 If you love me, you will obey what I command. And I will ask the Father, and he will give you another Counselor to be with you forever – the Spirit of truth. The world cannot accept him, because it neither sees him nor knows him. But you know him, for he lives with you and will be in you. I will not leave you as orphans; I will come to you.

Let's look at physical idols. The God of the Israelites is called the "Living God." Commandment number one: you will have no other gods before Me. Moses told the Israelites that when God spoke to them at Horeb, Mt. Sinai, they saw no form of any kind. God did not appear to them physically. God spoke to them out of the fire. Don't make idols for yourself because your God is a consuming fire, a jealous God. You don't make a shape and worship it – we have no idea what God looks like, so it is easy to worship Him by faith. God did that on purpose. We are not limited in our thinking of the things God can do for us because it is impossible to think of Him as too small. The things He did for Israel were huge.

Deuteronomy 4:15-19 You saw no form of any kind the day the Lord spoke to you at Horeb out of the fire. Therefore watch yourselves very carefully, so that you do not become corrupt and make for yourselves an idol, an image of any shape, whether formed like a man or a woman, or like any animal on earth or any bird that flies in the air, or like any creature that moves along the ground or any fish in the waters below. And when you look up to the sky and see the sun, the moon and the stars – all the heavenly array – do not be enticed into bowing down to them and worshiping things the Lord your God has apportioned to all the nations under heaven.

Isn't God awesome? He said to watch ourselves very carefully so that we don't become corrupt. If you lay your eyes on an object to pray to it, it is an idol. If you use an object to pray with, it is an idol. You will become corrupt. It doesn't matter who or what it is. If it is in the shape of anything, even Jesus, it is an idol. Praying to statues of Mary and Saints, stars, moons, etc. is idol worship. You have made them into false gods. Pinning amulets on idols for healing is obscene idol worship. By doing this you have become corrupt because you are putting your faith in objects instead of the one who heals you.

Exodus 15:26 He said, "If you listen carefully to the voice of the Lord your God and do what is right in his eyes, if you pay attention to his commands and keep all his decrees, I will not bring on you any of the diseases I brought on the Egyptians, for I am the Lord who heals you."

Psalm 103:2-3 Praise the Lord, O my soul, and forget not all his benefits – who forgives all your sins and heals all your diseases.

Deuteronomy 32:16 They made him jealous with their foreign gods and angered him with their detestable idols.

God gave us feelings and emotions, but the enemy uses them to lie to us if we are not careful. How can something made by the hands of man be a deity?

An idol is a carved image or amulet in any way, shape or form, made out of any material that you worship by talking to, praying to, bowing down to, kissing, making shrines for, depending on, hoping in, or trusting in, that takes the place of God. It can be a person, object or statue that you call on to do God's job. An idol is something or someone that takes the place of God in your life. A person can be an idol if you if you hold them in higher esteem than God. When you depend on another human being for your happiness, you have made them an idol. Lifestyle sins that you live in everyday are idols because you put them before God even though He told you in His Word that they are wrong and they remove you from His presence. You love the lifestyle more than God. God hates idols because He knows they are lies. We think of lies as being the least of all the sins. "Just a little white lie," we like to say but it is lying that got Satan kicked out of heaven. It is lying that started the fall of man in Eden and it is lying that will condemn us if we don't stop it. Jesus said Satan is the father of lies.

John 8:44 You belong to your father, the devil, and you want to carry out your father's desire. He was a murderer from the beginning, not holding to the truth, for there is no truth in him. When he lies, he speaks his native language, for he is a liar and the father of lies.

God made it so clear. Idols in any way, shape or form are lies. If it has a shape, do not worship it and do not use it for your worship.

Isaiah 44:6-20 "This is what the Lord says—Israel's King and Redeemer, the Lord Almighty: I am the first and I am the last; apart from me there is no God. Who then is like me? Let him proclaim it. Let him declare and lay out before me what has happened since I established my ancient people, and what is yet to come—yes, let them foretell what will come. Do not tremble, do not be afraid. Did I not proclaim this and foretell it long ago? You are my witnesses. Is there any God besides me? No, there is no other Rock; I know not one."

All who make idols are nothing, and the things they treasure are worthless. Those who would speak up for them are blind; they are ignorant, to their own shame. Who shapes a god and casts an idol, which can profit nothing? People who do that will be put to shame; such craftsmen are only human beings. Let them all come together and take their stand; they will be brought down to terror and shame.

The blacksmith takes a tool and works with it in the coals; he shapes an idol with hammers, he forges it with the might of his arm. He gets hungry and loses his strength; he drinks no water and grows faint. The carpenter measures with a line and makes an outline with a marker; he roughs it out with chisels and marks it with compasses. He shapes it in human form, human form in all its glory, that it may dwell in a shrine. He cut down cedars, or perhaps took a cypress or oak. He let it grow among the trees of the forest, or planted a pine, and the rain made it grow. It is used as fuel for burning; some of it he takes and warms himself, he kindles a fire and bakes bread. But he also fashions a god and

133

worships it; he makes an idol and bows down to it. Half of the wood he burns in the fire; over it he prepares his meal; he roasts his meat and eats his fill. He also warms himself and says, "Ah! I am warm; I see the fire." From the rest he makes a god, his idol; he bows down to it and worships. He prays to it and says, "Save me! You are my god!"

They know nothing, they understand nothing; their eyes are plastered over so they cannot see, and their minds closed so they cannot understand. No one stops to think, no one has the knowledge or understanding to say, "Half of it I used for fuel; I even baked bread over its coals, I roasted meat and I ate. Shall I make a detestable thing from what is left? Shall I bow down to a block of wood?"

Such a person feeds on ashes; a deluded heart misleads him; he cannot save himself, or say, "Is not this thing in my right hand a lie?"

Humans love to get touchy feely about stuff. We love security blankets. Idols are security blankets because you can see them and hold them and touch them. They are a source of contact for our feelings. They are things we can actually see to put our trust in. When we get emotionally in need, we like to hug and snuggle with anything. It can be a person or a pill, just something to make us feel better. Faith doesn't let you do that. God is to be our security blanket because He is alive and He saves, heals, and delivers. Idols do not. Faith in God requires you to snuggle with your Heavenly Father in the form of prayer and praise and worship. It requires that you read the Bible and build a relationship with God by faith. God doesn't need a shape to work in our lives and answer our prayers. He needs us to trust Him. Satan hates that because fellowship with God is worship. So he throws idols (lies) in our paths and we trip on them if we don't have a relationship with God. Obedience to God makes you strong. Your strength is in the Lord and "His" mighty power. The joy of the Lord is your strength. You don't need power of your own. You tap into His.

Ephesians 6:10 Finally, be strong in the Lord and in his mighty power.

Nehemiah 8:10 Nehemiah said, "Go and enjoy choice food and sweet drinks, and send some to those who have nothing prepared. This day is sacred to our Lord. Do not grieve, for the joy of the Lord is your strength."

Deuteronomy 7:5-6 This is what you are to do to them: Break down their altars, smash their sacred stones, cut down their Asherah poles and burn their idols in the fire. For you are a people holy to the Lord your God. The Lord your God has chosen you out of all the peoples on the face of the earth to be his people, his treasured possession.

God told Israel to completely destroy, break down, cut down, smash, burn and wipe out, every trace, all memory and every speck of idol worship that the nations they would dispose used in the worship of their gods. Even the very names of the idols were to be wiped out so there would be no memory of them.

You either follow God or you follow Satan. There is no in-between. If you don't follow either one, you follow Satan because you believe Satan's lies that there is neither God nor Satan.

Commandment number 1: Thou shalt have no other gods before Me. That commandment is pivotal in our walk and in our relationship with God. Idols cannot be a snare if they don't exist. Idols are a lie, get rid of them. Commandment number one wasn't enough. God knew it would have to be explained even farther in commandment number 2.

Exodus 20:4-6 You shall not make for yourself an idol in the form of anything in heaven above or on the earth beneath or in the waters below. You shall not bow down to them or worship them; for I the Lord your God, am a jealous God, punishing the children for the sin of the fathers to the third and fourth generation of those who hate me, but showing love to a thousand generations of those who love me and keep my commandments.

135

Deuteronomy 12:2-4 Destroy completely all the places on the high mountains and on the hills and under every spreading tree where the nations you are dispossessing worship their gods. Break down their altars, smash their sacred stones and burn their Asherah poles in the fire; cut down the idols of their gods and wipe out their names from those places. You must not worship the Lord your God in their way.

Don't just throw them away; destroy them. Break, smash, burn, cut down and wipe out! God is violent towards the enemy. The images of the stuff had to be totally and completely destroyed and every place the names were written had to be wiped clean so they would be forgotten forever. God does not want to be worshiped like that.

In Deuteronomy God told Israel ten very important things that still absolutely apply today because the same evil spirits are behind them.

Deuteronomy 7:25-26 The images of their gods you are to burn in the fire. Do not covet the silver and gold on them, and do not take it for yourselves, or you will be ensnared by it, for it is detestable to the Lord your God. Do not bring a detestable thing into your house or you, like it, will be set apart for destruction. Utterly abhor and detest it, for it is set apart for destruction.

1) *The images of the gods were to be burned in the fire.* Israel was to burn the images of the gods so they and their generations would not remember what those gods looked like and rebuild them and fall into idol worship. When you burn something there is nothing left to remember. You cannot put ash back together. There is no picture image to recreate and bring back. The memory of it is gone from the earth and from your mind and from your life. This is so important. Do not put things in front of your eyes that will stick in your mind and cause you to go after them and stumble: out of sight, out of mind. Keep your mind set on the things of God.

2) *Do not covet the silver and gold on the idols.* Don't wish it belonged to you. The gold and silver on the idols is worthless and polluted because it was given over to the enemy. It has become vile. Do not mourn its loss or its value because it is set apart for destruction and therefore it has no value. Don't covet the devil's stuff. Even though the gold and silver really belongs to God, (*The earth is the Lords and the fullness thereof. Psalm 24:1)* when God sees it, it is detestable to Him and He does not want it. The enemy in it is not hidden from Him.

3) *Do not take it for yourselves.* When you take it for your own, you will be joining yourself to it. You will become one with it. It will become your character. It is associated with you. When people see the item, they think of you. When they see you, they will think of the item. The idol will not become like you, you will become like the idol. Not because the idol is alive, but because the evil spirit behind it is. God does not want the enemy's stuff adorning His people. We are not to dress ourselves in the enemy's clothes. Burn it and destroy it.

Sometimes God would allow the people of Israel to take the plunder if the city was a distance from them. It could not be one of the nation's God was giving them as an inheritance (Deuteronomy 20:13-18). In these cities only, they could keep the silver and gold and stuff they found. But NEVER were they allowed to take for themselves the things devoted to idols and their worship. Those things were always utterly and completely destroyed. They were detestable in Gods eyes. The enemy they belonged to was trying to destroy God's people. God was protecting His people like loving parents protect their children.

4) *You will be ensnared by it.* "Trapped by a root that produces bitter poison." By keeping it you are making friends with the enemy. That root will wrap itself around your brain and you will begin to think about it and consider its ways and confusion will set in. How do you pledge allegiance to something that is dead

137

and doesn't love you? The idol is dead but the enemy behind it is not. You have believed his lie. It will trap you into believing the devils lies and you will forget about your God who loves you. Your eyes will be set on it and your faith in the true God will wane.

Deuteronomy 29:18 Make sure there is no man or woman, clan or tribe among you today whose heart turns away from the Lord our God to go and worship the gods of those nations; make sure there is no root among you that produces such bitter poison.

5) <u>*It is detestable to the Lord your God.*</u> The Lord is your God, not the idol. It is God who saves you, heals you, protects you and loves you. God hates idol worship so much that he destroyed every living thing in entire nations because of them. God hates idols because they are a lie from the enemy and they will keep you out of heaven. Since God hates them and we belong to God, we hate them, too. Our allegiance is to God.

6) <u>*Do not bring a detestable thing in your house.*</u> This is not hard. It is not ok to use idols as decorations in your homes. It is not ok to collect pagan gods because they are records of history. This also applies to pornography, astrology, drugs, witchcraft etc. That is another lie from the enemy. Your children will ask about them. They will research it and learn about them because they are curious. How can they learn faith when they are staring at an idol? That is just what the enemy wants. When you bring idols into your house, you are creating a relationship with the enemy. He is the very one that God sacrificed His only Son to save you from. Don't think for a minute that this does not apply to us today. It is detestable to God and because we belong to Him, it is detestable to us, too. It doesn't matter if you don't believe in them. If it is something that God hates, don't bring it home. You fill in the blank. What do you have in your house that God hates? If it is in your house, you have given the enemy permission to reap havoc in your home with his lies. Get it out. This is how you

decided in your heart that you will serve God only. This is how you use your freedom of choice to do God's will and not your own.

1 Samuel 15:29 He who is the Glory of Israel does not lie or change his mind; for he is not a man, that he should change his mind.

Psalm 101:2, 3 I will be careful to lead a blameless life – when will you come to me? I will walk in my house with blameless heart. I will set before my eyes no vile thing.

7) *You, like it, will be set apart for destruction.* God has already decided its destiny and its destiny is utter destruction. By bringing it into your house you join yourself to it. You and your house will be set apart for destruction with it. God is not only going to get rid of the thing, He is going to get rid of you, too, so it doesn't go any farther.

8) *Utterly abhor.* God not only told Israel what to do with the stuff, but also how to feel about it. Abhor it! But that wasn't enough. They had to "utterly" abhor it. The word "abhor" means to hate, but it has the added meaning of rejection. God didn't say just reject it. He said to completely, totally, and utterly reject it. Hate everything about it and everything it stands for. Know without a doubt that it is wrong and in error. Don't like even one little part about an idol. Reject the enemy of God and everything he stands for by removing the idol. Hate it and destroy it so you will not be ensnared by it. Know right away that your attitude about idols and anything to do with them is complete hate and rejection of what they stand for, absolutely no compromise. "My allegiance is to God alone. I have no desire to worship anything or anyone else so I will not set the enemies stuff before my eyes. I will not contaminate my household with the presence of any kind of idol. I will not grieve my God."

9) _Detest it._ Loathe it. Hate it. Want no part of it. If you hate it, you won't decorate your house with it.

10) _It is set apart for destruction._ It has already been decided that these detestable things will be destroyed. Destruction is its destiny. It has no future.

You don't take the devil's stuff and make something out of it for God. You don't copy the way of idol worship and turn it around and try and make it work for God and then expect God to be pleased with it. God doesn't need or want the devil's leftovers.

Isaiah 44:9-11 All who make idols are nothing, and the things they treasure are worthless. Those who would speak up for them are blind; they are ignorant, to their own shame. Who shapes a god and casts an idol, which can profit him nothing? He and his kind will be put to shame; craftsmen are nothing but men. Let them all come together and take their stand; they will be brought down to terror and infamy.

Remember temptation and the second right after the thought and how quickly you have to deal with it? The Israelites had not even seen the things they were to destroy yet. God was making it easy for them. They didn't have to worry about the temptation of what to do with the detestable things when they got there. Hate it now so when you get there you don't have to wonder about it. Prepare your hearts and eyes and minds now to utterly and completely hate and destroy the detestable things that you have not even seen yet. God was showing them how to beat the enemy. You can master the temptation because your attitude has already been set. When you get there you will know what to do and it will be easy for you. But there was even more.

Deuteronomy 12:30-32 And after they have been destroyed before you, be careful not to be ensnared by inquiring about their gods, saying, "How do these nations serve their gods? We will do the same." You must not worship the Lord your God in their way, because in worshiping

140

their gods, they do all kinds of detestable things the Lord hates. They even burn their sons and daughters in the fire as sacrifices to their gods. See that you do all I command you; do not add to it or take away from it.

Did God cover every angle or what? Destroy the people, destroy all of the idol stuff, wipe out the names and then don't ask about them. God covered the eyes of temptation and now He covers the mouth and the ears of temptation. The Israelites were told not even to ask about the way the nations served their gods. If they did, they would be ensnared. Just by asking! There it is again, temptation trying to get in your mind and heart by way of your eyes and ears. Don't spend even one second with the enemy by thinking about it, because when you do, you will be playing with temptation. Sin will definitely set in so don't invite the temptation. You master sin by not asking. It is much easier to not invite the temptation now than it is to get rid of it later. God told them how He wanted to be worshiped. They could not make it up themselves in any old way. "Do not add to or take away from anything I have commanded you. Do exactly what I told you."

After Israel had completely destroyed the nations before them, even though the people were gone, Israel would be tempted by what was left over. They were going to see evidence of idol worship. God said, "You are going to look at it and you are going to want to know how the people served their gods. It is going to look cool. The enemy has made it very attractive and you will want to incorporate it into your own style of worship and make it yours somehow because you can see and touch it, but you had better not! I just destroyed these nations because of this stuff. You do not use the enemy's stuff to worship me. You worship Me the way I taught you with praise on your lips and with full hearts and raised hands. You do not need objects or stuff to worship Me. Do not make statues of Me. I do not need a shape."

God warned Israel over and over again to destroy evil. Even though the people who practiced idolatry were dead and gone, Satan was not. His spirit was still alive and well in the articles and places of idol worship left behind. God was telling His people, "The enemy wants to mess you up and mess up My plans for you, but you are not to even wonder about it. You are not to ask questions about it or spend time looking at it. Walk away from the temptation. You cannot even use little pieces or parts of the things related to idol worship. Not the beads, gold or silver or pretty, brightly colored ribbons. You cannot use them in your worship or prayers or as decorations in your homes. God cannot be in the presence of evil. If your children see them, they will inquire about them. You are supposed to be teaching your children about Me, not idols. Destroy everything related to idol worship completely because if you don't you will be ensnared by them. It will trap you and it will get tangled up in your worship and in your belief system. It will become a stronghold and you will be no better than the peoples you disposed."

The Bible tells us in John 10:10 that the thief comes to kill, steal and destroy. And yet you want to use his tools to worship God. It is a search and destroy mission. You do not need the enemies help in your worship. You cannot mix the two up. Mastering sin applies here. Get rid of the temptations. Nowhere in the Bible does God give us physical items to use in our worship or to pray with and nowhere in the Bible does God tell us to use the pagan holidays to win others to Christ. What are we doing? We are supposed to be set apart and made holy for the Master's use. We are in this world but we are not of it. If we want to attract attention, we need to be different. Israel sure was.

Leviticus 20:26 You are to be holy to me because I the Lord am holy, and I have set you apart from the nations to be my own.

Don't you think it is noteworthy that the nations, who were totally given over to idol worship, were totally and completely given over? They had no problem being absolutely loyal to their detestable gods. Fake gods that could not save, heal, deliver or answer prayers. False gods they handmade themselves out of wood and stone that have no ears, eyes or brains and yet the people worshiped them and sacrificed their sons and daughters to them. The nations that worshiped worthless idols didn't cheat on their idols and wander off to God. And yet Israel who had seen God's deliverance over and over again wandered off to idols. It's baffling unless you know the spirit behind them. These nations said yes to Satan and opened the doors to temptation and were destroyed. They could have chosen God but they didn't. God did not get rid of the nations because Israel was so great, but because the nations were so absolutely wicked (Deuteronomy 9:4-6).

Exodus 33:16 "How will anyone know that you are pleased with me and with your people unless you go with us? What else will distinguish me and your people from all the other people on the face of the earth?"

Exodus 34:10 Then the Lord said (to Moses): "I am making a covenant with you. Before all your people I will do wonders never before done in any nation in all the world. The people you live among will see how awesome is the work that I, the Lord, will do for you."

Do you see? The people of Israel were watching God and the other nations were watching Israel. You talk about different! There was a pillar of cloud by day and a pillar of fire at night. They won battles without lifting a finger. Waters parted for them. God could have had a very big boat waiting, but He split the sea instead. When did God ever try to blend in? You don't be like everyone else to get noticed. If we want to get noticed and draw attention, our churches need to be different. The love of our supernatural God should be our visible different normal. That is how you get people in. The Holy Spirit in us is very attractive to the world and that is why Satan tries to make the world attractive to God's people. If Satan can get Israel to mess up, everyone will see. If he can get our churches to look like the world, then we just blend in. Satan does the opposite of what God does. God said to come out of the world and be separate. The enemy uses worldly things to draw us away from God. God said not to murder, Satan

143

says to kill our babies because it's really not a baby yet. God said a man will join a woman and become one flesh and Satan says if its love you can do whatever you want. The cross of Christ brought peace and it has been said that the peace sign is an upside down cross with broken arms. There is nothing like a ruined testimony. God said to worship Him with all your heart and Satan wants us to worship him by following the way of the world. It is a very long list of opposites. When your testimony is ruined, it not only defaces you, but it renders God a lie. All sin is idol worship.

When did an idol ever promise to love us or do wonders for us or take care of us? Why is it so hard to obey God and so easy to obey the enemy? If we are completely sold out to God, it's not hard at all. It is easy to obey the enemy when we don't have God's truth in us. The battle is only in the decision making once you learn the truth. Evil wants us to think that life in Christ is hard. The hardest part is deciding that you want to do what God says. Once you make the decision, you just have to stick with it. Then when the enemy starts placing his stuff before your eyes and ears, you turn around and walk away from the fence line, rejoicing because you have learned to master sin and reject temptation. The joy of the Lord is your strength. The other side of evil is awesome.

The God of Abraham, Isaac and Jacob was visible in His own way. Not only to Israel, but also to the nations around them. God was visible not in physical form, but in the miracles He did. A pillar of fire by night and a cloud by day, water from rocks, manna, victory over their enemies, shoes that never wore out. The nations were terrified of Israel's God. The Israelites had a personal relationship with their God. Why wasn't God enough? How is it that Israel was so intent on adopting idol worship? Why is evil so much more attractive than holiness? This is why: it has to do with our eyes and faith. You can't see faith. That's why the enemy loves to set his stuff in front of our eyes. Your eyes easily wrap themselves around objects and your mind blindly follows if

144

you let it. It happens when we are weak. That is obedience to the flesh. But faith corrects your eyesight. Faith tells your eyes the truth about what you are seeing and brings your mind into the obedience of Christ. There is no selfishness in faith. Faith is about God, not me. Faith trusts, hopes and believes what it cannot see.

Hebrews 11:1 Now faith is being sure of what we hope for and certain of what we do not see.

Hebrews 11:5-6 By faith Enoch was taken from this life, so that he did not experience death; he could not be found, because God had taken him away. For before he was taken, he was commended as one who pleased God. And without faith it is impossible to please God, because anyone who comes to him must believe that he exists and that he rewards those who earnestly seek him.

John 4:23 "Yet a time is coming and has now come when the true worshipers will worship the father in spirit and truth, for they are the kind of worshipers the Father seeks. God is sprit, and his worshipers must worship in spirit and in truth."

Jesus said that. We are to worship in spirit and truth. Get rid of your props. They are idols. God did not give Israel an image or beads, or stuff and things to worship and pray with. God did not set anything before their eyes to worship. They brought the offerings and sacrifices that God told them to bring. They brought the fruit of their lips: praise and worship and the lifting of their empty hands. They gave God adoration and thanksgiving without visibly seeing Him and they did it God's way. God taught them how to worship Him in spirit and truth. In return, God put His wonderful miracles in front of their eyes.

The articles used in the temple were a picture and a type of the promised Messiah that would come. The temple was a place for God to meet with His people. The tabernacle in the desert, candlesticks, altars, table, lamp stands, bronze basin, incense (Exodus 30:1-37), gold plates, dishes, pitchers, bowls, first fruit offerings from the harvest, animal sacrifices, priestly garments, anointing oil, the ark of the covenant, the tent of meeting, the festivals, and the Sabbath. Listen carefully now. All these things belonged to God. They were used "for" worship not "to" worship. It was God's stuff made exactly how God told them to make it. All of those things point to Jesus. Because of sin, God could not meet with us in just any old way. He is too holy to look upon sin. We have to prepare our hearts to meet with Him.

Psalm 66:17-20 I cried out to him with my mouth; his praise was on my tongue. If I had cherished sin in my heart, the Lord would not have listened; but God has surely listened and heard my voice in prayer. Praise be to God who has not rejected my prayer or withheld his love from me?

It is important to notice that none of God's things were images. Let that soak in. Never did God tell us to make a likeness of anything to bow down to.

Exodus 20:4-6 "You shall not make for yourself an idol in the form of anything in heaven above or on the earth beneath or in the waters below. You shall not bow down to them or worship them; for I, the Lord your God, am a jealous God, punishing the children for the sin of the fathers to the third and fourth generation of those who hate me, but showing love to a thousand generations of those who love me and keep my commandments.

The Israelites had their own stuff. The money and gold and silver and jewels that the Israelites owned themselves were given to them by God and offered back to God as a freewill offering when he needed them. It was as their hearts prompted them that they were to give (Exodus 35:20-29). God does not force us to worship Him. But He will tell us how He wants to be worshiped. All of God's stuff was used by God to meet with His people. The things were holy. Even the fire was holy because God lit the fire Himself. Do you understand? God is not like any other god. You do not worship Him in your own way. You cannot come into the presence of God in just any old way. He is holy and His ways are holy. By Him we are made holy (Exodus 31:12-13). Everything we are belongs to God. That is what you do when you worship. You give yourself, your heart, mind and soul. God made your heart, mind, spirit and soul. He wants your willing, obedient heart. Your heart is the most valuable thing you can give to God because it is what He can work with to bring you close to Him. That is the war between good and evil in a nutshell. God does not need or want objects in your worship. Your statues, beads, altars, sacrifices, festivals, costumes, rabbit's feet and good luck charms: all the stuff and things that the enemy tries to fill our eyes and ears with to keep our hearts from God are of no value. They have nothing to do with your relationship with God and everything to do with the enemy. Our lives have nothing to do with "luck."

In Exodus 34:20 God says that no one is to appear before Him empty-handed. You take an offering with you because everything you have is His. That is worship, too. Your money is not to become an idol. When we finally stand before Him, we will lay the crowns that He gives us at His feet.

Here's the thing about idols. They are very convenient. You can package them however you want. If yours is small enough, you can put it in your pocket and take it with you. You have complete control over an idol. There is no accountability. They don't get mad and threaten to send you to hell because that would be rude and they are politically correct at all times. If you want, you can tie a string around their necks and use them for cat toys. They do not offend. Anything goes and no one gets hurt. They believe what you believe. You can make up whatever rules you want and personalize them just for you. Idols don't boss you around and tell you what you can and can't do. You get to be the boss. You tell them. You don't have to worry about faith when you are dealing with idols. You are the god of the idol. If one lets you down, you can snap its little head off and create another. You can see idols. You can make them as cute or fearsome as you

147

want. You can look at them when you are talking to them and if you are especially sad or needy, you can pick one up and hug it, adorable.

Did you notice? You do everything for the idol and it does nothing for you. You are actually the god of the idol. Finally you get to be the boss and call the shots. You are in control, but the idol will not help you or love you back. It is a lie. Idols are a vivid display of the ridiculousness of Satan. They are cold and unresponsive and empty. Objects of nothingness designed to keep your eyes off of your loving God and His Son Jesus who is the fullness of everything. We don't need anything else because God gave us Jesus to fill everything in every way.

Ephesians 1:22-23 And God placed all things under his feet and appointed him to be head over everything for the church, which is his body, in the fullness of him who fills everything in every way.

We who believe are the church and Jesus is the head over everything for the church, us. Why do you know God but you are living like you do? Why are you not wholly devoted to the One who loves you so much that He sent His only Son to die for your sins so you could live with Him forever? Why have you diluted your faith for your own satisfaction? Why are you not afraid of grieving your Creator?

The stone tablets that God wrote the Ten Commandments on were hidden in the Ark of the Covenant. They were to be obeyed not worshiped. The ark itself was placed behind the veil in the temple. Don't bow down to it. The priest could go in once a year to sprinkle blood on the atonement seat for the sins of the people. That's it. Then leave.

Now listen carefully. Our sacrifices of praise and worship and the giving of our hearts and our resources to God do not fall on blind eyes or deaf ears. Our love for God does not go unrewarded. He is the God who sees and hears. Why would you want to kneel before an idol? Why would you pray to anyone or anything other than God?

We are rewarded not only with the promise of heaven, but in our everyday lives, too. We don't pray for nothing. Prayer is a gift to us from God so that we can communicate with Him. He hears our prayers.

2 Chronicles 7:14 if my people, who are called by my name, will humble themselves and pray and seek my face and turn from their wicked ways, then will I hear from heaven and will forgive their sin and will heal their land.

2 Chronicles 30:27 The priests and the Levites stood to bless the people, and God heard them, for their prayer reached heaven, his holy dwelling place.

Ezra 8:23 So we fasted and petitioned our God about this, and he answered our prayer.

Psalm 66:20 Praise be to God, who has not rejected my prayer or withheld his love from me!

Psalm 141:2 May my prayer be set before you like incense; may the lifting up of my hands be like the evening sacrifice.

Proverbs 15:8 The Lord detests the sacrifice of the wicked, but the prayer of the upright pleases him.

Proverbs 15:29 The Lord is far from the wicked but he hears the prayer of the righteous.

Proverbs 28:9 If anyone turns a deaf ear to the law, even his prayers are detestable.

Ephesians 6:18 And pray in the Spirit on all occasions with all kinds of prayers and requests. With this in mind, be alert and always keep on praying for all the saints.

Philippians 4:6 Do not be anxious about anything, but in everything, by prayer and petition, with thanksgiving, present your requests to God.

James 5:16 Therefore confess your sins to each other and pray for each other so that you may be healed. The prayer of a righteous man is powerful and effective.

1 Peter 3:12 For the eyes of the Lord are on the righteous and his ears are attentive to their prayer, but the face of the Lord is against those who do evil.

Revelation 5:8 And when he had taken it, the four living creatures and the twenty-four elders fell down before the Lamb. Each one had a harp and they were holding golden bowls full of incense, which are the prayers of the saints.

Revelation 8:4 The smoke of the incense, together with the prayers of the saints, went up before God from the angel's hand.

The prayers of God's people are a fragrant incense before God. You had better believe the enemies of God do not want you to pray. That's why there is so much sin in the world to listen to and look at that will keep you away from holiness so you will forget God.

Sin is a root that produces bitter poison. One little seed of sin would produce a root that would entangle itself around the whole camp and poison it. It's the same today. Our Heavenly Father tells us we can't mess with the enemy or his stuff because he does bad things and causes us to do the same. We are told to throw fellow Christians out of the church who are rebellious because they become a type of yeast that works itself through the church. Others will look at them and say, "Oh, I didn't know it was OK with God for us to do that. I will do it too, then." Christ is misrepresented and the enemy becomes a stronghold in the church.

1 Corinthians 5:6-7 Your boasting is not good. Don't you know that a little yeast works through the whole batch of dough? Get rid of the old yeast that may be a new batch without yeast – as you really are. For Christ, our Passover Lamb, has been sacrificed.

1 Corinthians 5:9-12 I have written to you in my letter not to associate with sexually immoral people – not at all meaning the people of this world who are immoral, or the greedy and swindlers, or idolaters. In that case you would have to leave this world. But now I am writing you that you must not associate with anyone who calls himself a brother but is sexually immoral or greedy, an idolater or a slanderer, a drunkard or a swindler. With such a man do not even eat. What business is it of mine to judge those outside the church? Are you not to judge those inside? God will judge those outside. "Expel the wicked man from among you."

Psalm 63:3-5 Because your love is better than life, my lips will glorify you. I will praise you as long as I live, and in your name I will lift up my hands. My soul will be satisfied as with the richest of foods; with singing lips my mouth will praise you.

2 Corinthians 4:18 So we fix our eyes not on what is seen, but on what is unseen. For what is seen is temporary, but what is unseen is eternal.

2 Corinthians 5:7 We live by faith not by sight.

Romans 10:17 Faith comes by hearing and hearing by the word of God.

God had commanded Israel to remain faithful to Him. He was creating a whole new race of people. They were not to intermarry with the nations they were to dispose. They were a new bloodline belonging to God. Jesus would come from the nation of Israel. They could not get involved with the pagan traditions and false Gods of those nations and begin to follow them. God's way would be watered down, mixed up, confused and eventually disappear altogether.

151

Do not be unequally yoked. Do not join yourselves to idolaters. It is always the Christian who falls. Remember, it is a spiritual battle and evil spirits are strong. The goal of evil is to draw you away from salvation and to get your mind off your Creator. That is why God destroyed the nations of Canaan. The people were completely given over to idolatry. Their hearts would not change and their generations would continue in their detestable ways. God in His mercy waited until the "fullness of their sin" was complete because He was giving them every opportunity to repent. God gave them hundreds of years of mercy and a chance to repent. But they didn't so He wiped them out and gave Israel their land.

Deuteronomy 7:3-4 Do not intermarry with them. Do not give your daughters to their sons or take their daughters for your sons, for they will turn your sons away from following me to serve other Gods, and the Lord's anger will burn against you and will quickly destroy you.

Deuteronomy 20:18 Otherwise, they will teach you to follow all the detestable things they do in worshiping their gods, and you will sin against the Lord your God.

Deuteronomy 29:18 Make sure there is no man or woman, clan or tribe among you today whose heart turns away from the Lord our God to go and worship the gods of those nations; make sure there is no root among you that produces such bitter poison.

God told us how we should live in 66 books, 929 chapters, all contained in one book called the Bible. He warned us about the enemy. God told us what He would do for us if we obey Him and what the results would be if we did not obey Him. The entire Bible is filled with warnings and examples. From the first page of Genesis to the last page of Revelation, we are warned, we are promised and we are loved.

It is a supernatural book breathed upon by God. God does not lie. Everything God said in His Word is proved in your own life. Everything that is going on in the world today is proved in the Bible. God said it would happen and it is. If you don't read His book, you have no excuse for your ignorance or for you troubles or for your lack of faith. You cannot know who He is if you don't read the Bible and you will have no faith. Without faith, it is impossible to please Him. If you want to know the rules, read the book. Then go one step farther and obey it.

Chapter 7
The Army and the Breath of God

Matthew 4:4
Jesus answered, "It is written, 'Man does not live on bread alone, but on every word that comes from the mouth of God.'"

ehemiah 7:73-Nehemiah 8 The priests, the Levites, the gatekeepers, the singers and the temple servants, along with certain of the people and the rest of the Israelites, settled in their own towns.

When the seventh month came and the Israelites had settled in their towns, all the people assembled as one man in the square before the Water Gate. They told Ezra the scribe to bring out the Book of the Law of Moses, which the Lord had commanded for Israel. So on the first day of the seventh month Ezra the priest brought the Law before the assembly, which was made up of men and women and all who were able to understand. He read it aloud from daybreak till noon as he faced the square before the Water Gate in the presence of the men, women and others who could understand. And all the people listened attentively to the Book of the Law.

Ezra the scribe stood on a high wooden platform built for the occasion. Beside him on his right stood Mattithiah, Shema, Anaiah, Uriah, Hilkiah and Maaseiah; and on his left were Pedaiah, Mishael, Malkijah, Hashum, Hashbaddanah, Zechariah and Meshullam.

Ezra opened the book. All the people could see him because he was standing above them; and as he opened it, the people all stood up. Ezra praised the Lord, the great God; and all the people lifted their hands and responded, "Amen! Amen!" Then they bowed down and worshiped the Lord with their faces to the ground.

The Levites—Jeshua, Bani, Sherebiah, Jamin, Akkub, Shabbethai, Hodiah, Maaseiah, Kelita, Azariah, Jozabad, Hanan and Pelaiah—instructed the people in the Law while the people were standing there. They read from the Book of the Law of God, making it clear and giving the meaning so that the people could understand what was being read.

Then Nehemiah the governor, Ezra the priest and scribe, and the Levites who were instructing the people said to them all, "This day is sacred to the Lord your God. Do not mourn or weep." For all the people had been weeping as they listened to the words of the Law.

Nehemiah said, "Go and enjoy choice food and sweet drinks, and send some to those who have nothing prepared. This day is sacred to our Lord. Do not grieve, for the joy of the Lord is your strength."

Then all the people went away to eat and drink, to send portions of food and to celebrate with great joy, because they now understood the words that had been made known to them.

On the second day of the month, the heads of all the families, along with the priests and the Levites, gathered around Ezra the scribe to give attention to the words of the Law. They found written in the Law, which the Lord had commanded through Moses, that the Israelites were to live in booths during the feast of the seventh month and that they should proclaim this word and spread it throughout their towns and in Jerusalem: "Go out into the hill country and bring back branches from olive and wild olive trees, and from myrtles, palms and shade trees, to make booths"—as it is written.

So the people went out and brought back branches and built themselves booths on their own roofs, in their courtyards, in the courts of *the house of God and in the square by the Water Gate and the one by the Gate of Ephraim. The whole company that had returned from exile built booths and lived in them. From the days of Joshua son of Nun until that day, the Israelites had not celebrated it like this. And their joy was very great.*

Day after day, from the first day to the last, Ezra read from the Book of the Law of God. They celebrated the feast for seven days, and on the eighth day, in accordance with the regulation, there was an assembly.

Have you ever been so happy you cried? This has been a very long haul for the Israelites. They left Egypt, got to the door of their promise, had to turn around, wandered in the desert for forty years, finally entered their promised land, got kicked out of their promised land, the temple and the palaces were completely destroyed by fire, the people were taken captive in Babylon for 70 years, and now they have returned to their land. After much opposition from their enemies, they have completed the wall with God's supernatural help in fifty-two days.

Nehemiah 6:15-16 So the wall was completed on the twenty-fifth of Elul, in fifty-two days. When all our enemies heard about this, all the surrounding nations were afraid and lost their self-confidence, because they realized that this work had been done with the help of our God.

The enemies of Israel had not forgotten the God of Israel. Israel has not forgotten their God either. They have gathered as one man the Bible says. That means they all have the same heart. They are not divided as men, women or leaders. There is no king; only Nehemiah the Governor and servant of God who led the remnant of Israel to rebuild the walls and who restored order. They are just a unified people hungry for the breath of God. They miss God. It is the people who tell Ezra the scribe to bring out the Book of the Law of Moses and read it to them. He read from day-break till noon and all the people listened attentively to the words of God, given to them through Moses so long ago. As Ezra opened the book, all the people stood up. That is reverence for God. We should still do that.

Psalm 126:1-3 When the Lord brought back the captives to Zion, we were like men who dreamed. Our mouths were filled with laughter, our tongues with songs of joy. Then it was said among the nations, "The Lord has done great things for them." The lord has done great things for us, and we are filled with joy.

This is huge! It is the first day of the seventh month. Seven is God's number for completeness. Israel has come full circle. They are weeping as they listen to the words being read to them because they know that it is their sin that has caused their afflictions. They see how they have rebelled against God and their hearts are filled with grief. But this is not a day for weeping. God has forgiven them and this is a day of rejoicing. Don't grieve because the joy of the Lord is your strength.

On the second day of the month the heads of the families and the priests and the Levites gathered around Ezra to hear more. Then they took what they heard and proclaimed it throughout the towns and in Jerusalem. But they didn't just read the law, they obeyed it and their joy was very great.

Jeremiah 15:16 When your words came, I ate them; they were my joy and my heart's delight, for I bear your name, O Lord God Almighty.

The Book of the Law of Moses is the first five books of the Old Testament. We get to read them too: Genesis, Exodus, Leviticus, Numbers and Deuteronomy. We can weep and rejoice with Israel because the joy of the Lord is our strength. We are the children of Abraham along with Israel. Because of Jesus, we have been grafted in.

Galatians 3:29 If you belong to Christ, then you are Abraham's seed, and heirs according to the promise.

Ephesians 3:6 This mystery is that through the gospel the Gentiles are heirs together with Israel, members together of one body, and sharers together in the promise in Christ Jesus.

Gentiles are heirs together with Israel because of the gospel. The gospel is the message of Jesus. It is the first four books of the New Testament: Matthew, Mark, Luke and John. And really, the whole story of the Bible.

Oh the precious, fragrant, life giving breath of God. When we read the Bible, it is like we are being breathed on again and again. The breath of God is alive. When God speaks, what He says will happen. God cannot lie. The same breath that created the earth and all living things, the same breath that breathed life into man speaks to us through His living, breathed on Word and we are changed. No wonder the people cried. As God's words were being read to them they could see their sin. They could hear the forgiveness of God and were filled with His love. They had finally returned to their promised land and there was joy. We have finally returned to our loving Creator when we are saved and He breathes new life into us and our willing spirits obey Him. The key is to have a willing spirit.

Psalm 51:10-12 Create in me a pure heart, O God, and renew a steadfast spirit within me. Do not cast me from your presence or take your Holy Spirit from me. Restore to me the joy of your salvation and grant me a willing spirit, to sustain me.

Before Jerusalem was destroyed for her disobedience and fell into captivity, something odd happened. An eight year old named Josiah became king. It was not his age that was odd, it was his heart. Listen to what the Bible says about Josiah's grandfather and father:

2 Kings 21:10-11 The Lord said through his servants the prophets: "Manasseh king of Judah has committed these detestable sins. He has done more evil than the Amorites who preceded him and has let Judah into sin with his idols.

2 Kings 21:19-22 Amon was twenty-two years old when he became king, and he reigned in Jerusalem two years. His mother's name was Meshullemeth daughter of Haruz; she was from Jotbah. He did evil in the eyes of the Lord, as his father Manasseh had done. He walked in all the ways of his father; he worshiped the idols his father had worshiped, and bowed down to them. He forsook the Lord, the God of his fathers, and did not walk in the way of the Lord.

2 Kings 21:26 He was buried in his grave in the garden of Uzza. And Josiah his son succeeded him as king.

This is what the Bible says about the eight year old Josiah:

2 Kings 22:1-2 Josiah was eight years old when he became king, and he reigned in Jerusalem thirty-one years. His mother's name was Jedidah daughter of Adaiah; she was from Bozkath. He did what was right in the eyes of the Lord and walked in all the ways of his father David, not turning aside to the right or to the left.

How did that happen? His father and grandfather were evil. Maybe his mother taught him about God, the Bible doesn't tell us. But Josiah has a heart for God. He did what was right in God's eyes and he didn't look to the left or right. That means no compromise. When he was 26, he started repairing the temple of the Lord. That is when the Book of the Law was found by Hilkiah the high priest.

2 Kings 22:8 Hilkiah the high priest said to Shaphan the secretary, "I have found the Book of the Law in the temple of the Lord." He gave it to Shaphan, who read it.

2 Kings 22:10-11 Then Shaphan the secretary informed the king, "Hilkiah the priest has given me a book." And Shaphan read from it in

160

the presence of the king. When the king heard the words of the Book of the Law, he tore his robes.

That is a heart that is broken for God. Josiah had never read the Book of the Law before. Its words pierced his heart because his heart recognized God in what he was hearing. He listens as Shaphan reads of the disaster that is coming on Israel because of her disobedience. It is a genuine fear of the Lord that causes him to do what he did next.

2 Kings 22:12-13 He gave these orders to Hilkiah the priest, Ahikam son of Shaphan, Acbor son of Micaiah, Shaphan the secretary and Asaiah the king's attendant: "Go and inquire of the Lord for me and for the people and for all Judah about what is written in this book that has been found. Great is the Lord's anger that burns against us because our fathers have not obeyed the words of this book; they have not acted in accordance with all that is written there concerning us."

Do you see his heart? Like Moses, Josiah is concerned not only for himself but for the people of Judah. He is concerned because they have not been obeying the law. Now he wants to hear from God about what to do. Tearing his robes was a symbol of humility before God. God is King. He is not proud or arrogant and he is not going to step out on his own without inquiring of the Lord first. God honors Josiah's heart and gives him the following message:

2 Kings 22:14-20 Hilkiah the priest, Ahikam, Acbor, Shaphan and Asaiah went to speak to the prophetess Huldah, who was the wife of Shallum son of Tikvah, the son of Harhas, keeper of the wardrobe. She lived in Jerusalem, in the Second District.

She said to them, "This is what the Lord, the God of Israel, says: Tell the man who sent you to me, 'This is what the Lord says: I am going to bring disaster on this place and its people, according to everything written in the book the king of Judah has read. Because they have forsaken me and burned incense to other gods and provoked me to anger by all the idols their hands have made, my anger will burn against this place and will not be quenched.' Tell the king of Judah, who sent you to inquire of the Lord, 'This is what the Lord, the God of Israel, says concerning the words you heard: Because your heart was responsive and you humbled yourself before the Lord when you heard what I have spoken against this place and its people, that they would become accursed and laid waste, and because you tore your robes and wept in my presence, I have heard you, declares the Lord. Therefore I will gather you to your fathers, and you will be buried in peace. Your eyes will not see all the disaster I am going to bring on this place.'"

So they took her answer back to the king.

Josiah could have said, "Well, I'm safe, whew!" But his heart was responsive and filled with God's words and he got to work. The first order of business was to get all the people together so they will know what is going on. Just like the Levites in Nehemiah, Josiah read the Book of the Law to everyone. He opened his mouth and used the sword of the Spirit out loud against the enemy and it permeated the hearts of all the people. Now everyone is on the same page. That is what we need to do in our families.

2 Kings 23:1-3 Then the king called together all the elders of Judah and Jerusalem. He went up to the temple of the Lord with the men of Judah, the people of Jerusalem, the priests and the prophets—all the people from the least to the greatest. He read in their hearing all the words of the Book of the Covenant, which had been found in the temple of the Lord. The king stood by the pillar and renewed the covenant in the presence of the Lord—to follow the Lord and keep his commands, regulations and decrees with all his heart and all his soul, thus confirming the words of the covenant written in this book. Then all the people pledged themselves to the covenant.

The living, breathed on, words of God were read out loud to all the people from the least to the greatest. The precious breath of God covered His people. It was a very important first order of

162

business. They renewed the covenant in God's presence to obey the Lord. There must be unity to get the work done. There has to be oneness of heart to make the changes that were coming. Get this in you! It is as fresh today as it was back then.

Jeremiah 23:29 "Is not my word like fire," declares the Lord, "and like a hammer that breaks a rock in pieces?"

2 Timothy 3:14-17 But as for you, continue in what you have learned and have become convinced of, because you know those from whom you learned it, and how from infancy you have known the holy Scriptures, which are able to make you wise for salvation through faith in Christ Jesus. All Scripture is God-breathed and is useful for teaching, rebuking, correcting and training in righteousness, so that the man of God may be thoroughly equipped for every good work.

Do you remember what God told the Israelites to do with the enemy idol stuff before they started to take the promised land?

Deuteronomy 7:5-6 This is what you are to do to them: Break down their altars, smash their sacred stones, cut down their Asherah poles and burn their idols in the fire. For you are a people holy to the Lord your God. The Lord your God has chosen you out of all the peoples on the face of the earth to be his people, his treasured possession.

This is what Josiah is reading to the people. They get it and that is exactly what Josiah did. He cleaned up Judah and set his house in order according to the exact words of the law. He didn't destroy some things and leave others for later. He was responsive and humble before his God. God said that. We should listen to Him. When we respond to His words and humble ourselves, He moves in our behalf. Read it again.

2 Kings 22:19-20 Because your heart was responsive and you humbled yourself before the Lord when you heard what I have spoken against this place and its people, that they would become accursed and laid waste, and because you tore your robes and wept in my presence, I have heard you, declares the Lord. Therefore I will gather you to your fathers, and you will be buried in peace. Your eyes will not see all the disaster I am going to bring on this place.'"

1 Samuel 15:29 He who is the Glory of Israel does not lie or change his mind; for he is not a man, that he should change his mind."

Judgment would still come to Israel because of her unfaithfulness, but Josiah would not have to see it.

2 Kings 23:4-26 The king ordered Hilkiah the high priest, the priests next in rank and the doorkeepers to remove from the temple of the Lord all the articles made for Baal and Asherah and all the starry hosts. He burned them outside Jerusalem in the fields of the Kidron Valley and took the ashes to Bethel. He did away with the pagan priests appointed by the kings of Judah to burn incense on the high places of the towns of Judah and on those around Jerusalem—those who burned incense to Baal, to the sun and moon, to the constellations and to all the starry hosts. He took the Asherah pole from the temple of the Lord to the Kidron Valley outside Jerusalem and burned it there. He ground it to powder and scattered the dust over the graves of the common people. He also tore down the quarters of the male shrine prostitutes, which were in the temple of the Lord and where women did weaving for Asherah.

Josiah brought all the priests from the towns of Judah and desecrated the high places, from Geba to Beersheba, where the priests had burned incense. He broke down the shrines at the gates—at the entrance to the Gate of Joshua, the city governor, which is on the left of the city gate. Although the priests of the high places did not serve at the altar of the Lord in Jerusalem, they ate unleavened bread with their fellow priests.

He desecrated Topheth, which was in the Valley of Ben Hinnom, so no one could use it to sacrifice his son or daughter in the fire to Molech. He removed from the entrance to the temple of the Lord the horses that the kings of Judah had dedicated to the sun. They were in the court near the room of an official named Nathan-Melech. Josiah then burned the chariots dedicated to the sun.

He pulled down the altars the kings of Judah had erected on the roof near the upper room of Ahaz, and the altars Manasseh had built in the two courts of the temple of the Lord. He removed them from there, smashed them to pieces and threw the rubble into the Kidron Valley. The king also desecrated the high places that were east of Jerusalem on the south of the Hill of Corruption—the ones Solomon king of Israel had built for Ashtoreth the vile goddess of the Sidonians, for Chemosh the vile god of Moab, and for Molech the detestable god of the people of Ammon. Josiah smashed the sacred stones and cut down the Asherah poles and covered the sites with human bones.

Even the altar at Bethel, the high place made by Jeroboam son of Nebat, who had caused Israel to sin—even that altar and high place he demolished. He burned the high place and ground it to powder, and burned the Asherah pole also. Then Josiah looked around, and when he saw the tombs that were there on the hillside, he had the bones removed from them and burned on the altar to defile it, in accordance with the word of the Lord proclaimed by the man of God who foretold these things.

The king asked, "What is that tombstone I see?"

The men of the city said, "It marks the tomb of the man of God who came from Judah and pronounced against the altar of Bethel the very things you have done to it."

"Leave it alone," he said. "Don't let anyone disturb his bones." So they spared his bones and those of the prophet who had come from Samaria.

Just as he had done at Bethel, Josiah removed and defiled all the shrines at the high places that the kings of Israel had built in the towns of Samaria that had provoked the Lord to anger. Josiah slaughtered all the priests of those high places on the altars and burned human bones on them. Then he went back to Jerusalem.

The king gave this order to all the people: "Celebrate the Passover to the Lord your God, as it is written in this Book of the Covenant." Not since the days of the judges who led Israel, nor throughout the days of the kings of Israel and the kings of Judah, had any such Passover been observed. But in the eighteenth year of King Josiah, this Passover was celebrated to the Lord in Jerusalem.

165

Furthermore, Josiah got rid of the mediums and spiritists, the household gods, the idols and all the other detestable things seen in Judah and Jerusalem. This he did to fulfill the requirements of the law written in the book that Hilkiah the priest had discovered in the temple of the Lord. Neither before nor after Josiah was there a king like him who turned to the Lord as he did—with all his heart and with all his soul and with all his strength, in accordance with all the Law of Moses.

Nevertheless, the Lord did not turn away from the heat of his fierce anger, which burned against Judah because of all that Manasseh had done to provoke him to anger. So the Lord said, "I will remove Judah also from my presence as I removed Israel, and I will reject Jerusalem, the city I chose, and this temple, about which I said, 'There shall my Name be.'"

Josiah was on a search and destroy mission! After he destroyed, he looked around for more. "What else needs to go? What else do you hate, Lord?" Josiah was zealous for God. He had the zeal of the Lord in his heart. 2 Chronicles 34 tells us he began to seek God when he was sixteen years old. When he was eighteen, he started to get rid of the idols in Judah and Jerusalem. He was only twenty six years old when he began to repair the temple. It is not your age that determines how much God can use you, it is your heart. It is your willingness to obey God no matter what. Josiah's father and grandfather were kings who led Israel into sin. The people of Israel did not have to follow, but they did. They made the conscious decision to disobey God and obey their evil kings. Judgment was coming.

Josiah was building his house and his city on a rock. Its foundations were firmly set on the Word of God. He celebrated the Passover exactly as God instructed in the Book of the Law.

2 Chronicles 35:18 The Passover had not been celebrated like this in Israel since the days of the prophet Samuel; and none of the kings of Israel had ever celebrated such a Passover as did Josiah, with the priests, the Levites and all Judah and Israel who were there with the people of Jerusalem.

There was never a king like Josiah the Bible says. He did everything God said in the Book of the Law. He is a perfect example of how our hearts should be towards God and his Word. Josiah reigned for thirty-one years. Four evil kings later, the judgment of God came upon Judah and Jerusalem and they fell just as God said. The walls were broken down and the temple and the palaces burned. Everything of value was destroyed. Then the people went into captivity in Babylon for seventy years and the land rested.

The Israelites Book of the Law is not for today's Christians to keep. It was for Israel at that time. The Old Testament promises and the New Testament delivers. We are under a new covenant. Instead of written laws, we have the Holy Spirit in us to convict us of our sins. The law is written on our hearts.

Jeremiah 31:31-32 "The time is coming," declares the Lord, "when I will make a new covenant with the house of Israel and with the house of Judah. It will not be like the covenant I made with their forefathers when I took them by the hand to lead them out of Egypt, because they broke my covenant, though I was a husband to them," declares the Lord. "This is the covenant I will make with the house of Israel after that time," declares the Lord. "I will put my law in their minds and write it on their hearts. I will be their God, and they will be my people."

Hebrews 9:15 For this reason Christ is the mediator of a new covenant, that those who are called may receive the promised eternal inheritance – now that he has died as ransom to set them free from the sins committed under the first covenant.

Luke 22:20 In the same way, after the supper he took the cup, saying, "This cup is the new covenant in my blood, which is poured out for you."

Romans 10:4 Christ is the end of the law so that there may be righteousness for everyone who believes.

The issue that has not changed is our obedience. But how do we be obedient?

Galatians 5:16-18 So I say, live by the Spirit, and you will not gratify the desires of the sinful nature. For the sinful nature desires what is contrary to the Spirit and the Spirit what is contrary to the sinful nature. They are in conflict with each other, so that you do not do what you want. But if you are led by the Spirit, you are not under law.

Romans 12:2 Do not conform any longer to the pattern of this world, but be transformed by the renewing of your mind. Then you will be able to test and approve what God's will is – his good, pleasing and perfect will.

Romans 12:9-16 Love must be sincere. Hate what is evil; cling to what is good. Be devoted to one another in brotherly love. Honor one another above yourselves. Never be lacking in zeal, but keep your spiritual fervor, serving the Lord. Be joyful in hope, patient in affliction, faithful in prayer. Share with God's people who are in need. Practice hospitality. Bless those who persecute you; bless and do not curse. Rejoice with those who rejoice; mourn with those who mourn. Live in harmony with one another. Do not be proud, but be willing to associate with people of low position. Do not be conceited.

1 Peter 1:23 For you have been born again, not of perishable seed, but of imperishable, through the living and enduring word of God.

Psalm 119:9-16 How can a young man keep his way pure? By living according to your Word. I seek you with all my heart; do not let me stray from your commands. I have hidden your word in my heart that I might not sin against you. Praise be to you O Lord; teach me your decrees. With my lips I recount all the laws that come from your mouth. I rejoice in following your statutes as one rejoices in great riches. I meditate on your precepts and consider your ways. I delight in your decrees; I will not neglect your word.

2 Timothy 3:14-15 But as for you, continue in what you have learned and have become convinced of, because you know those from whom you learned it, and how from infancy you have known the holy Scriptures, which are able to make you wise for salvation through faith in Christ Jesus.

What? Back up…. *"and how from infancy you have known the holy Scriptures, which are able to make you wise for salvation."* Have our children known the Holy Scriptures from infancy so they can be wise for salvation? Do you read the Bible to your children at home every day so they will build a relationship with God? When was the last time you were in church and saw children? They are all in the nursery or separated into their own groups. Our kids are out of church for elementary school, junior high, high school and college. No wonder they don't go to church anymore as adults. They never went as children! No wonder they don't know how to worship. This is not good. This teaches our kids that they don't belong in church. They learn to stay out of church. You can hear them playing on the playground during service. They don't know how to sit still and listen. Church is not a "got to go." It is a "get to go." It is a privilege. It should be vastly different from any other event in their week. We separate the marrieds from the singles, the men from the women, the children from the adults and even the children from the children and we wonder why the unity is gone and our families stray. Children don't worship with their parents because it is strange to them. Israel came with their children to meet with God to hear His Word. They stood up while the Word of God was being read to them. They were building a relationship with God. Now we excuse them before the service to go on Easter egg hunts! It's appalling. Our children miss spoken words of God and being in His presence. They miss the stories of their salvation to go play.

There is no relationship and there is no reverent fear of the Lord in them.

2 Kings 17:33 They worshiped the Lord, but they also served their own gods in accordance with the customs of the nations from which they had been brought.

2 Kings 17:41 Even while these people were worshiping the Lord, they were serving their idols. To this day their children and grandchildren continue to do as their fathers did.

Church is where families gather together to worship and hear from God. We are building a relationship with our Creator. There should be a holy reverence for the Bible. Children need to know what it feels like to be breathed on by the spoken Word of God. They need to know what it is like to be in His presence so when they are out of His presence they will recognize what is missing. Like the Israelites when Ezra read the holy words of God to the people, we need to assemble as one people to hear not just one verse, but whole chapters of the Bible. If you want to be with God, if you want to hear from Him, go where He hangs out. Go to His Word.

Joshua 8:35 There was not a word of all that Moses had commanded that Joshua did not read to the whole assembly of Israel, including the women and children, and the aliens who lived among them.

Deuteronomy 31:12-13 Assemble the people – men, women and children, and the aliens living in your towns – so they can listen and learn to fear the lord your God and follow carefully all the words of this law. Their children, who do not know this law, must hear it and learn to fear the Lord your God as long as you live in the land you are crossing the Jordan to possess.

Hebrews 4:12 For the word of God is living and active. Sharper than any double-edged sword, it penetrates even to dividing soul and spirit, joints and marrow; it judges the thoughts and attitudes of the heart.

170

We have to get to the place in our hearts where no matter what happens, we trust God. No matter how much we want something, we obey God instead. How can we get to that place if we don't read His words? How can we change the attitude of our heart if we don't fill it with God's stuff?

Psalm 1:1-3 Blessed is the man who does not walk in the counsel of the wicked or stand in the way of sinners or sit in the seat of mockers. But his delight is in the law of the Lord and on his law he meditates day and night. He is like a tree planted by streams of water, which yields its fruit in season and whose leaf does not wither. Whatever he does prospers.

Isaiah 55:10-11 As the rain and the snow come down from heaven, and do not return to it without watering the earth and making it bud and flourish, so that it yields seed for the sower and bread for the eater, so is my word that goes out from my mouth: It will not return to me empty, but will accomplish what I desire and achieve the purpose for which I sent it.

Deuteronomy 30:11-14 Now what I am commanding you today is not too difficult for you or beyond your reach. It is not up in heaven, so that you have to ask, "Who will ascend into heaven to get it and proclaim it to us so we may obey it?" Nor is it beyond the sea, so that you have to ask, "Who will cross the sea to get it and proclaim it to us so we may obey it?" No, the word is very near you; it is in your mouth and in your heart so you may obey it.

In Matthew Jesus taught us how to build our house. We do it by not just hearing His words, but by actually putting them into practice. It is a wise man who builds his house upon the rock of Jesus and His words. Then when the enemy strikes, when disaster hits, we will not fall. To fall means to back away from God: to give up on Him and abandon our faith. But our foundation is built on Jesus our Rock, on the living breathed on words of God. When the terrible happens, the world says, "Why

171

did God let this happen? If there really were a God, He would not have let this happen." As Christians we can turn this around and say, "We were ready. The enemy was not victorious in my family because we belong to God. Greater is He that is in me than He that is in the world. God provided once and He will provide again. I will see my loved ones again. I trust you God and having done all; I will stand on your living, breathed on Word."

Ephesians 6:13 Therefore put on the full armor of God, so that when the day of evil comes, you may be able to stand your ground, and after you have done everything, to stand.

Romans 8:35-39 Who shall separate us from the love of Christ? Shall trouble or hardship or persecution or famine or nakedness or danger or sword? As it is written: "For your sake we face death all day long; we are considered as sheep to be slaughtered." No, in all these things we are more than conquerors through him who loved us. For I am convinced that neither death nor life, neither angels nor demons, neither the present nor the future, nor any powers, neither height nor depth, nor anything else in all creation, will be able to separate us from the love of God that is in Christ Jesus our Lord.

The tragedy of the house built upon the sand is the hopelessness of the fall. Where do you go for comfort? How do you find peace? Who will rebuild your house? Who will repair your broken heart? Jesus said the foolish man built his house on the sand and it fell with a great crash.

Matthew 7:24-29 (KJV) Therefore whosoever heareth these sayings of mine, and doeth them, I will liken him unto a wise man, which built his house upon a rock: And the rain descended, and the floods came, and the winds blew, and beat upon that house; and it fell not: for it was founded upon a rock. And every one that heareth these sayings of mine, and doeth them not, shall be likened unto a foolish man, which built his house upon the sand: And the rain descended, and the floods came, and the winds blew, and beat upon that house; and it fell: and great was the fall of it. And it came to pass, when Jesus had ended these sayings, the people were astonished at his doctrine: For he taught them as one having authority, and not as the scribes.

Deuteronomy 32:3-4 I will proclaim the name of the Lord. Oh, praise the greatness of our God! He is the Rock, his works are perfect, and all his ways are just. A faithful God who does no wrong, upright and just is he.

Leviticus 18:5 Keep my decrees and laws, for the person who obeys them will live by them. I am the Lord.

Psalm 19:8-11 The precepts of the Lord are right, giving joy to the heart. The commands of the Lord are radiant, giving light to the eyes. The fear of the Lord is pure, enduring forever. The ordinances of the Lord are sure and altogether righteous. They are more precious than gold, than much pure gold; they are sweeter than honey from the comb. By them is your servant warned; in keeping them there is great reward.

Psalm 119:97-104 Oh , how I love your law! I meditate on it all day long. Your commands make me wiser than my enemies, for they are ever with me. I have more insight than all my teachers, for I mediate on your statutes. I have more understanding than the elders, for I obey your precepts. I have kept my feet from every evil path so that I might obey your word. I have not departed from your laws, for you yourself have taught me. How sweet are your words to my taste, sweeter than honey to my mouth! I gain understanding from your precepts; therefore I hate every wrong path.

The enemy does not want you to know that the foolish man can become wise; that the house that fell with a great crash can be rebuilt on a new foundation found in Christ our rock. He doesn't want you to know that there is hope and healing in the precious, wonderful, fragrant breath of God. He doesn't want you to build a relationship with God because he wants you to serve him. But the house of Satan is built on sand. When the rains come down and the streams rise, when the wind blows and beats against his house, it will fall with a great crash never to rise again and he knows it.

Revelation 20:10 And the devil, who deceived them, was thrown into the lake of burning sulfur, where the beast and the false prophet had been thrown. They will be tormented day and night for ever and ever.

Revelation 20:15 If anyone's name was not found written in the book of life, he was thrown into the lake of fire.

There is a book in the hands of God in which is written the names of those that belong to Jesus. It is called the Lambs Book of Life. It has many pages with lots and lots of room for your name. But never let anyone tell you that your name cannot be blotted out because you chose sin instead.

Exodus 32:33 The Lord replied to Moses, "Whoever has sinned against me I will blot out of my book."

Psalm 9:5 You have rebuked the nations and destroyed the wicked; you have blotted out their names for ever and ever.

Revelation 3:4-6 Yet you have a few people in Sardis who have not soiled their clothes. They will walk with me, dressed in white, for they are worthy. He who overcomes will, like them, be dressed in white. I will never blot out his name from the book of life, but will acknowledge his name before my Father and his angels. He who has an ear, let him hear what the Spirit says to the churches.

Are you listening?

Chapter 8
THE ARMY IN THE GARDEN

James 2:19
You believe that there is one God. Good! Even the demons believe that —
and shudder.

D id you know Satan was the very first fence-line jumper?
Everything was fine until the first thought entered into
his head. We don't know how long he entertained the
thought, but he probably mulled it around for a long time. After
all, this wasn't just anyone he was about to rebel against. How do
you tell God you want His job? Surely he must have known that
God would know what he was thinking.

Proverbs 15:3 The eyes of the Lord are everywhere keeping watch on
the wicked and the good.

Psalm 147:5 Great is our Lord and mighty in power; his
understanding has no limit.

God knew Satan was talking to the angels about rebelling
with him. God already had everything figured out before Satan

and the angels rebelled. His plan was already in place before creation. The Bible tells us that angels rebelled with Satan. Talk about your fence line decisions affecting those around you? This one not only affected heaven, but the whole world for all time. When we knowingly sin, we are jumping over the fence line and joining the angels that rebelled with Satan. Does that make sin a little clearer?

Satan entertained the temptation of pride and rebellion because he wanted to be God and he wanted to be worshiped. Sin loves company so he got other angels to consider the temptation, too. They all made the final decision to go for it and dove over the fence line. The first sin was a lie in heaven. No wonder God hates lying so much. This is what Jesus said about Satan to the Pharisees:

John 8:44 "You belong to your father, the devil, and you want to carry out your father's desire. He was a murderer from the beginning, not holding to the truth, for there is no truth in him. When he lies, he speaks his native language, for he is a liar and the father of lies."

Remember the yeast and the pure church (1 Corinthians 5:6-8)? That is what was happening in heaven. The yeast spread throughout the angels. If it can happen in heaven, it can happen in your home and in your church. If they got kicked out of heaven, we will too. The penalty was and still is separation from God and eternity in hell. Eternity means forever.

Matthew 25:45-46 "He will reply, 'I tell you the truth, whatever you did not do for one of the least of these, you did not do for me.' Then they will go away to eternal punishment, but the righteous to eternal life."

Jude 1:7 In a similar way, Sodom and Gomorrah and the surrounding towns gave themselves up to sexual immorality and perversion. They serve as an example of those who suffer the punishment of eternal fire.

God kicked them all out of heaven. How terrifying for an angel to be separated from God and how terrifying for the angels in heaven to see what happened to the ones who chose to leave.

Jude 1:6 And the angels who did not keep their positions of authority, but abandoned their own home—these he has kept in darkness, bound with everlasting chains for judgment on the great Day.

Satan got kicked out of heaven, but he is not done yet. He decides to focus his attention on God's creation. What better place than the earth. But God is not done yet either. His plan is perfect and nothing can mess it up.

To really understand sin, we have to go back to the Garden of Eden. God planted the Garden and there were lots of trees, but there were two specific trees in the middle. You know what they are: The tree of life and the tree of the knowledge of good and evil. There was only one of each.

Genesis 2:8-9 Now the Lord God had planted a garden in the east, in Eden; and there he put the man he had formed. The Lord God made all kinds of trees grow out of the ground – trees that were pleasing to the eye and good for food. In the middle of the garden were the tree of life and the tree of the knowledge of good and evil.

When God made the earth and everything on it He did so with "Let there be." The earth and the animals and plants were all spoken into existence. But when God created man it was different.

Genesis 1:26 Then God said, "Let us make man in our image, in our likeness, and let them rule over the fish of the sea and the birds of the air, over the livestock, over all the earth, and over all the creatures that move along the ground."

Genesis 2:7 (KJV) And the Lord God formed man of the dust of the ground, and breathed into his nostrils the breath of life; and man became a living soul.

Man was made in the image of God. God formed man with His own hands and breathed His own breath into him. The breath of God is in our DNA! We didn't lose that in the garden. That is why even the soul of an atheist longs for the things of God. He has the very breath of God in him and there is nothing he can do about it.

Genesis 2:15-17 The Lord God took the man and put him in the Garden of Eden to work it and take care of it. And the Lord God commanded the man, "You are free to eat from any tree in the garden; but you must not eat from the tree of the knowledge of good and evil, for when you eat from it you will certainly die."

Then God made Eve and somewhere along the line she was told the same thing about the trees. Just like us, they have to choose to love God and obey Him. They could eat from all the trees in the garden including the fruit of the tree of life. The only one they could not eat of was the tree of the knowledge of good and evil. They did fine until the enemy tricked Eve. It worked in heaven with the angels so now Satan is going to mess up God's "man." Man has been given the authority that Satan wants.

Psalm 8:3-9 When I consider your heavens, the work of your fingers, the moon and the stars, which you have set in place, what is man that you are mindful of him, the son of man that you care for him? You made him a little lower than the heavenly beings and crowned him with glory and honor. You made him ruler over the works of your hands; you put everything under his feet: all flocks and herds, and the beasts of the field, the birds of the air, and the fish of the sea, all that swim the paths of the seas. O Lord, our Lord, how majestic is your name in all the earth!

Isn't that what Satan always wanted: to be worshiped and to lord over his own world?

Matthew 4:8-10 Again, the devil took him to a very high mountain and showed him all the kingdoms of the world and their splendor. "All

178

*this I will give you," he said, "if you will bow down and worship me."
Jesus said to him, "Away from me, Satan! For it is written: 'Worship
the Lord your God, and serve him only.'"*

Satan could hardly believe there was a "man." Now God's
"man" gets to lord over the earth. Not if Satan can help it. He
approached Adam and Eve as one of their own creatures in Eden
and lied to them. Temptation wants you to get as close as possible
to the sin, remember? See it, smell it, touch it, then pick it. That's
when you are at the fence line. You can still beat the temptation
by dropping the fruit and running away. All you have to do to
jump the fence is eat it. That is complete acceptance of the sin.

*Genesis 3:1-2 Now the serpent was more crafty than any of the wild
animals the Lord God had made. He said to the woman, "Did God really
say, 'You must not eat from any tree in the garden?'" The woman said
to the serpent, "We may eat fruit from the trees in the garden, but God
did say, 'You must not eat fruit from the tree that is in the middle of the
garden, and you must not touch it, or you will die.'"*

Why did Eve say that? God didn't say they couldn't touch
the fruit. He said you cannot eat the fruit. Just being in the
presence of evil, sin was having its way. You could look at it,
touch it, pick it, toss it back and forth, play with it, rub it, sniff it,
peel it and cut it up in little pieces if you wanted to. That's how
temptation gets you to the fence-line. But you could not eat it
because God said "no." If you ate it you would disobey God and
jump over the fence line and suffer the consequences. By eating it,
you would become one with it and would be participating in its
effects and be separated from God. That's exactly why the Bible
tells us not to hang out with sin. You will become like it. Stay
away from the temptation.

*Genesis 3:4 "You will not certainly die," the serpent said to the
woman, "For God knows that when you eat from it your eyes will be
opened, and you will be like God, knowing good and evil."*

Do you hear the lie? "You're not going to die. God is lying because He doesn't want you to be like Him and know things." Can you see Satan's hidden agenda? "Be like God," he said. That's what Satan wanted. His deceit was effective on the angels in heaven and now it would work on God's man in the garden.

Genesis 3:6-13 When the woman saw that the fruit of the tree was good for food and pleasing to the eye, and also desirable for gaining wisdom, she took some and ate it.

She set her eyes on it, considered it, rationalized about it, touched it and picked it. She spent too much time with temptation. Remember, at the fence line, you don't think about why not; only how can I? Then instead of running, she ate it. She did not re-consider anything God told her. Wasn't it fast? Then she turns to Adam and gives him some and just five sentences it was done. We tend to forget that Adam was there, too, engaged in the same temptation. He didn't get involved in the conversation, but he focused his eyes and ears on the temptation so when the time came, he was ready to jump over the fence line with Eve.

She also gave some to her husband, who was with her and he ate it. Then the eyes of both of them were opened, and they realized they were naked; so they sewed fig leaves together and made coverings for themselves. Then the man and his wife heard the sound of the Lord God as he was walking in the garden in the cool of the day, and they hid from the Lord God among the trees of the garden. But the Lord God called to the man, "Where are you?" He answered, "I heard you in the garden, and I was afraid because I was naked; so I hid." And he said, "Who told you that you were naked? Have you eaten from the tree that I commanded you not to eat from?" The man said, "The woman you put here with me – she gave me some fruit from the tree, and I ate it." Then the Lord God said to the woman, "What is this you have done?" The woman said, "The serpent deceived me, and I ate."

Satan's lie to Eve was the first sin on earth. Eating the fruit was the first sin on earth by man. Now the devil has messed with things in heaven and on earth. The separation from God was instant. That is spiritual death. The first consequence was knowledge and immediately after was fear. Is God surprised at all of this? No. How do we know? First, the two trees were already in the Garden of Eden before God put man there (Genesis 2:15). The plan was already in place. Second, God told Adam and Eve what would happen if they didn't do what He said. He said, "You will die." He was talking about a spiritual death: separation from God. He had already been there with the heavenly hosts. He didn't have to make something up at the last minute. By the time Adam and Eve came along it was a no-brainer. God had everything settled in heaven and on earth even before the angels fell. God told Eve that her seed, Jesus, would crush the head of Satan. God had a plan.

Genesis 3:15 And I will put enmity between you and the woman, and between your offspring and hers; he will crush your head, and you will strike his heel."

The enemy of man may strike and bruise, but in the end he will be crushed. Now Adam and Eve know what sin is. Their eyes have been opened and they know they are naked, so they hide from God. Blame is flying all over the place. Adam blames God for the woman. He blames the woman for the fruit. The woman blames the snake for lying to her. Disobedience bears fruit and every one of us has sin nature today because of that one act. The tree could have had fruit that could not be touched like Eve told Satan. But that was not what God said. He said not to eat the fruit. You don't get the benefit of the trees without eating the fruit. Eating the fruit of these two trees bore unique results offered by no other tree in the garden. To live forever: eat the fruit of the tree of life. To die a spiritual death and be separated from God: eat the fruit of the tree of the knowledge of good and evil.

The fruit had to be consumed. The sin was very specific. Do not eat the fruit.

Adam and Eve had God's spirit in them; the breath of life. After they ate the fruit, they had sin nature in them, too, because of the act of their disobedience. This is very important. God did not make man with sin nature. Adam and Eve were perfect until they made their choice to sin and eat the fruit. You cannot say, "Well, God made me this way" as justification for your sin. We have sin nature in us as a result of Adam and Eve's sin in the garden, not because God made us that way. Just as we choose to sin, we have to choose to be changed. Now their offspring know the difference between good and evil, too. The sweet innocence of Adam and Eve and all mankind was lost forever.

Genesis 3:22 And the Lord God said, "The man has now become like one of us, knowing good and evil. He must not be allowed to reach out his hand and take also from the tree of life and eat, and live forever."

Before sin entered in, Adam and Eve could eat from the tree of life and live forever in God's perfect, beautiful garden. It wasn't a problem. But sin cannot dwell with God in heaven and sin is not allowed to live forever. So like the angels who rebelled, Adam and Eve die a spiritual death and are separated from God. They can no longer live in His presence. God took away the tree of Life and the beautiful garden, and man was separated from God that very day. The tree of the knowledge of good and evil is never mentioned again. Its purpose was accomplished. What a shock it must have been for Adam and Eve. When they got up that morning everything was wonderful. By the afternoon they are kicked out of the Garden of Eden and headed towards the same end as the fallen angels, except for one thing. Man has been given a way out. The blood of Jesus would purchase our salvation and make a way for us to be in God's presence again. The only thing they had to do was repent and obey God.

Are you seeing the pattern? God kicks sin out of heaven. God kicks sin out of Eden. God kicks sin out of Adam and Eve's family when Cain killed Able. God kicks sin off of the earth by the flood. God tells the Israelites they must purge, kick out, the evil from among them. God kicked sin out of His Tabernacle in the desert. God kicks sin out of Canaan so His people can live there. Jesus kicked sin out of the temple in Jerusalem. God tells us in the New Testament to kick sin out of the church. We are warned to kick sin out of our hearts, and in Revelation we come full circle when He kicks all sin off the earth and warns us that sin will not be allowed in heaven. Do you understand why? It is because God Himself lives in all those places: heaven, Eden, earth, His temple, the Ark of the Covenant, Canaan, our churches and our hearts. He is too holy to be in the presence of sin, but He wanted to be with us so badly He made a way by covering Himself with clouds, smoke, fire, curtains, rocks and finally, permanently, by the blood of His very own Son. We think God wants for us to make a way to be with Him, and yet throughout all of history every story is about God making a way to be with us. God is very much with us and what He desires is relationship.

Psalm 46:1 God is our refuge and strength, an ever-present help in trouble.

Psalm 46:7 The Lord Almighty is with us; the God of Jacob is our fortress.

Remember what Jesus said on the cross before He died? "It is finished." That was the plan of God from the very beginning. The cross of Christ is how God beat sin. Jesus is the seed of Eve that would crush the head of Satan. Now it is accomplished and we have to wait to live with God again until the judgment when Satan and sin will be destroyed forever. Then we will have access to the tree of life once more. In the meantime, the way we live our lives will show God if we belong to Him or the enemy. Just as Adam and Eve chose to sin and ate the fruit, we have to choose the fruit of righteousness and believe in Jesus and accept what He did on the cross for us. Then we have to obey. God can be with us and we can be with God because of the cross.

Philippians 1:10-11 So that you may be able to discern what is best and may be pure and blameless until the day of Christ, filled with the fruit of righteousness that comes through Jesus Christ—to the glory and praise of God.

Mankind is connected to each other by sin nature which was placed in Adam and Eve when they ate the fruit and passed sin nature on to us through procreation. It is impossible for us to be perfect like Adam and Eve before the fall. Babies are not born perfect. They have sin nature in them from birth. We are all Adam's seed.

Genesis 8:21 The Lord smelled the pleasing aroma and said in his heart: "Never again will I curse the ground because of man, even though every inclination of his heart is evil from childhood. And never again will I destroy all living creatures, as I have done.

Romans 3:23 For all have sinned and fall short of the glory of God,

Out of evil comes God's discipline, but He never leaves us there. The fruit of the tree was also the knowledge of good; the fruit of God's wisdom and grace. Man was not left alone to figure all this out on his own. Everything man is about is tied to the cross of Christ. We have been given God's wisdom so we can understand what God has freely given us so if we choose it, we may be redeemed.

1 Corinthians 1:27-31 But God chose the foolish things of the world to shame the wise; God chose the weak things of the world to shame the strong. He chose the lowly things of this world and the despised things—and the things that are not—to nullify the things that are, so that no one may boast before him. It is because of him that you are in Christ Jesus, who has become for us wisdom from God—that is, our righteousness, holiness and redemption. Therefore, as it is written: "Let him who boasts boast in the Lord."

1 Corinthians 2:6-16 We do, however, speak a message of wisdom among the mature, but not the wisdom of this age or of the rulers of this age, who are coming to nothing. No, we speak of God's secret wisdom, a wisdom that has been hidden and that God destined for our glory before time began. None of the rulers of this age understood it, for if they had, they would not have crucified the Lord of glory. However, as it is written: "No eye has seen, no ear has heard, no mind has conceived what God has prepared for those who love him" but God has revealed it to us by his Spirit.

The Spirit searches all things, even the deep things of God. For who among men knows the thoughts of a man except the man's spirit within him? In the same way no one knows the thoughts of God except the Spirit of God. We have not received the spirit of the world but the Spirit who is from God, that we may understand what God has freely given us. This is what we speak, not in words taught us by human wisdom but in words taught by the Spirit, expressing spiritual truths in spiritual words. The man without the Spirit does not accept the things that come from the Spirit of God, for they are foolishness to him, and he cannot understand them, because they are spiritually discerned. The spiritual man makes judgments about all things, but he himself is not subject to any man's judgment: "For who has known the mind of the Lord that he may instruct him?" But we have the mind of Christ.

It may not seem like it, but it was just perfect. What a wonderful, wonderful plan! No wonder God put the tree of the knowledge of good and evil in the garden. He knew man would fall. By eating the fruit, God's perfect plan of salvation was in place. His own Son Jesus would come to earth as all God and all man and would die on the cross one time to include all the sins of all man for all time. Then He gave us His Holy Spirit so we would understand the secret things of God. Satan thought man was doomed when Adam and Eve ate the fruit. Satan thought man would live in hell with him. But the fruit of sin nature connects us all so that the blood of Jesus could cover us all, once and for all.

1 Corinthians 15:22 For as in Adam all die, so in Christ all will be made alive.

Salvation is already there for all of us, we just have to lay hold of it. That is our free gift. Just as sin is a choice, so is salvation. We didn't have a choice about the sin nature in us. But we do have the choice to have Jesus in us. We have a choice to be saved, or not.

John 3:16 For God so loved the world that he gave his one and only Son, that whoever believes in him shall not perish but have eternal life.

Matthew 11:12 From the days of John the Baptist until now, the kingdom of heaven has been forcefully advancing, and forceful men lay hold of it.

Hebrews 7:23-27 Now there have been many of those priests, since death prevented them from continuing in office; but because Jesus lives forever, he has a permanent priesthood. Therefore he is able to save completely those who come to God through him, because he always lives to intercede for them. Such a high priest meets our need—one who is holy, blameless, pure, set apart from sinners, exalted above the heavens. Unlike the other high priests, he does not need to offer sacrifices day after day, first for his own sins, and then for the sins of the people. He sacrificed for their sins once for all when he offered himself.

Matthew 3:8 Produce fruit in keeping with repentance.

Matthew 7:20 Thus, by their fruit you will recognize them.

Satan unwittingly used the fruit of the tree of the knowledge of good and evil to separate us from God so we would join him and the fallen angels in hell. He had no idea that God created the fruit of the tree of the knowledge of good and evil to include fallen man in His wonderful salvation plan. There is no salvation in place for the angels who sinned. Satan and the fallen angels do not have a way back into heaven, but we do. Can you imagine being an angel who followed Satan? The angels remember what heaven was like. They remember what it was like to be in the presence of God. They know they blew it. They cannot change their minds and repent and go back to their heavenly home. But we can. The gift of eternity in heaven with God by way of the cross is only for fallen man; but only if he accepts it and then obeys.

2 Corinthians 5:10 For we must all appear before the judgment seat of Christ, that each one may receive what is due him for the things done while in the body, whether good or bad.

Jesus died once for all sins forever. That includes the unsaved. He doesn't have to die again every time someone changes their mind and decides that Jesus is indeed Lord. But redemption does not take effect until you open your mouth and eat the fruit of the cross by asking Jesus into your heart and repenting of your sins. If you want to be redeemed, snatched out of the enemy's hand, you must become a child of God. You do that by asking Jesus into your heart. Get it? You need Jesus in you. Jesus nullifies the sin nature consequences of the ancient fruit. Is it any wonder that God calls consequences fruit?

Psalm 104:13 He watereth the mountains from his chambers and the earth is filled with the fruit of thy works.

Proverbs 11:30 The fruit of the righteous is a tree of life, and he who wins souls is wise.

Proverbs 18:21 The tongue has the power of life and death, and those who love it will eat its fruit.

Isaiah 3:10 Tell the righteous it will be well with them, for they will enjoy the fruit of their deeds.

187

Why is all of this important? Because we cannot go to heaven dressed in our presumptuous, willful sin even if we believe in God and the Holy Spirit and Jesus and the cross. Jesus said He would not recognize us (Matthew 7:21-23). God tells the church in His Word to wash their robes so they will have the right to go into heaven.   We cannot be in His presence clinging to our sin; especially when He forewarned us. It will not happen. This makes the world angry, but isn't it better to get rid of sin than continue in it? Isn't that why we have so many clinics out there trying to help people clean up the messes they are in? Think of God and His Word, "The Holy Bible" as a clinic. It's free and it works if you obey it. God Himself is your counselor and He really loves you and wants you to succeed. Since He is the one who made you, He knows how to fix you. Let's look at some of the sins the Bible says will keep us out of heaven.

Presumptuous sin: The Christian says; "I'm safe! We were born like this with sin nature so it is impossible to be perfect. God knows my heart and that it is good. Besides, I believe that Jesus died for me so I don't have to worry about my sins anymore; once saved, always saved. I am free to sin because Jesus will forgive me anyway no matter what I do." *(Psalm 6:14-16, Psalm 19:13, Isaiah 57:17, Ezekiel 18:24, Matthew 7:21-23, Galatians 5:13, Hebrews 10:26-31, Colossians 3:5-10)*

The sin of sexual immorality: "We love each other and are really committed to each other so God doesn't mind if we live together because we are married in our hearts. It's OK if we sleep together sometimes because we will marry someday. Casual sex is OK anyway as long as no one gets hurt. Who cares what I do in the privacy of my home?" *(Leviticus 18, Ezekiel 18:24, Ephesians 5:11, 1 Corinthians 6:12-20, 1 Thessalonians 4:3-8, Hebrews 10:26-31, 12:16, 13:4, Colossians 3:5-10)*

The sin of homosexuality: "I was born this way and God loves me just as I am. God made me like this." Or, "The ones I loved hurt me so I will try homosexuality to see if I can find the love I am looking for there." *(Leviticus 18:22, Leviticus 20:13, Ezekiel 18:24, 1 Corinthians 6:9-11, 18-19, 6:18-20, Romans 1:24-32, Galatians 5:19-21, 1 Thessalonians 4:3-8, Hebrews 10:26-31, Colossians 3:5-10)*

The sin of drunkenness: "But I was born this way and I can't help it. It is an inherited disease after all. It is embedded in my DNA. Jesus drank wine." *(Isaiah 5:11-12, Proverbs 20:1, Proverbs 23:20-21, Proverbs 23:29-35, Ezekiel 18:24, Luke 21:33-36, 1 Corinthians 5:11-12, 1 Corinthians 6:9-11, Galatians 5:19-21, Ephesians 5:15-18, Colossians 3:5-10, 1 Peter 4:1-7, Hebrews 10:26-31)*

The sin of sorcery (drugs): "I have an addictive personality. I was born with it." Or, "I can't quit. I use to cover the pain, God understands." "I'm just having fun. God knows my heart is good towards Him." *(Deuteronomy 18:10-14, Hebrews 10:26-31, Isaiah 47:12-15, Colossians 3:5-10, Revelation 21:8, Revelation 22:15)*

The sin of witchcraft: Horoscope, palm reading, cards, fortune telling, tea leaves, etc. *(Leviticus 19:26, 31, Leviticus 20:6, 27, Deuteronomy 18:10-12, Hebrews10:26-31, Galatians 5:19-21, Colossians 3:5-10)*

The sin of being lukewarm: People say, "I am not a bad person. I don't cheat people or steal or murder. I don't go to church, but God knows my heart is good. I believe there is a God, but I'm not sure about the Jesus thing. You don't have to go to church to go to heaven." *(John 1:10-13, John 3:16-21, Hebrews 10-25, Colossians 3:5-10, Revelation 3:15-16)*

The sin of idolatry: "But my statues and the things I use to worship with, are all for God." *(Exodus 20:4, Isaiah 44:6-20, Jeremiah 7:30, 44:3-5, Ephesians 5:5, Colossians 3:5-10)*

The sin of the unsaved world: "You must love and accept everyone just as they are. It is time the Church evolves with the

189

rest of the world and starts to practice tolerance and acceptance of everyone. The world is different now and the Bible needs to catch up. If there is a God, He made everyone just as they are and we should all love each other no matter how we are born." *(1 Thessalonians 4:3-8, 2 Thessalonians 1:5-9, Romans 1:18-20, Colossians 3:5-10)*

But Jesus said, "You must be born again."

John 3:3-6 In reply Jesus declared, "I tell you the truth, no one can see the kingdom of God unless he is born again." "How can a man be born when he is old?" Nicodemus asked. "Surely he cannot enter a second time into his mother's womb to be born!" Jesus answered, "I tell you the truth, no one can enter the kingdom of God unless he is born of water and the Spirit. Flesh gives birth to flesh, but the Spirit gives birth to spirit."

Isaiah 55:6-9 Seek the Lord while he may be found; call on him while he is near. Let the wicked forsake his way and the evil man his thoughts. Let him turn to the Lord, and he will have mercy on him, and to our God, for he will freely pardon. "For my thoughts are not your thoughts, neither are your ways my ways," declares the Lord. "As the heavens are higher than the earth, so are my ways higher than your ways and my thoughts than your thoughts."

Ezekiel 18:24 "But if a righteous man turns from his righteousness and commits sin and does the same detestable things the wicked man does, will he live? None of the righteous things he has done will be remembered. Because of the unfaithfulness he is guilty of and because of the sins he has committed, he will die."

It may be a different world, but sin is still the same. We got our sin nature from Adam and Eve who got it from Satan himself. That is why it is not OK to be who you are with what you were born with. You were not born perfect like Adam and Eve were when God made them. God did not create sin and He did not make you like you are with sin-nature. God loves you but He hates your sin. That is why we have to choose to be born again and change our ways.

God's Word doesn't have to evolve to fit in with the world. It was perfect from the very beginning. The world has not evolved. It has eroded. It has grown away from God. It has turned into a cesspool of sin that has been declared legal by man. Now man wants to rewrite God's Word to give approval to the sins man wants to freely commit. Isn't it odd that the unsaved world wants the church to agree with them? It is not enough to change the laws. It is not enough to win approval from the media or from man. The approval or peace of mind doesn't seem to be official until the church agrees. That is because Satan is involved. Whether you are saved or not, you were created in the image of God and you have a spirit. Your spirit knows and longs for God's presence. That is the emptiness so many people talk about who don't have a relationship with God.

Adam and Eve and the fallen angels and Satan himself all believed in God and still they were kicked out of His presence because of their sin. The only way back is faith in the blood of Jesus and Jesus is only available to man.

1 Samuel 15:22-23 But Samuel replied: "Does the Lord delight in burnt offerings and sacrifices as much as in obeying the voice of the Lord? To obey is better than sacrifice, and to heed is better than the fat of rams. For rebellion is like the sin of divination, and arrogance like the evil of idolatry. Because you have rejected the word of the Lord, he has rejected you as king."

When you sin, you are in defiance of the authority of God. You are telling God that you will take over now because you know better than Him and you do not like what He told you to do. You are listening to the people around you because they agree with you and give you permission to sin.

Romans 1:32 Although they know God's righteous decree that those who do such things deserve death, they not only continue to do these very things but also approve of those who practice them.

Psalm 12:8 The wicked freely strut about when what is vile is honored among men.

They try to make you feel OK about what you are doing, but it doesn't work. It doesn't work because the approval of man does not influence the Holy Spirit inside you. The Holy Spirit will never be pacified by the approval of man. You will never find peace and happiness in your sin. Your soul is on God's side, so what you feel inside is war between your flesh and your soul. Your soul is your mind, will and emotions. You spirit is your character and your personality. Your flesh is the part of you that doesn't want to obey God (Galatians 5:19-21).

1 Peter 1:9 For you are receiving the end result of your faith, the salvation of your souls.

Proverbs 11:30 (KJV) The fruit of the righteous is a tree of life; and he that winneth souls is wise.

The soul that has been won is the soul (mind, will and emotions) that has decided that Jesus is Lord and seeks to obey God.

The only thing that will quiet your soul (mind, will and emotions) is the presence of God. Drugs and alcohol will not drown the longing of your soul to be with God. Human love and acceptance will not cover over the longing of your soul to be in the presence of God.

1 Peter 2:11 Dear friends, I urge you, as aliens and strangers in the world, to abstain from sinful desires that wage war against your soul.

If the angels in heaven didn't get away with sin, neither will we.

Psalm 103:20-22 Praise the Lord, you his angels, you mighty ones who do his bidding, who obey his word. Praise the Lord, all his heavenly hosts, you his servants who do his will. Praise the Lord, all his works everywhere in his dominion. Praise the Lord, O my soul.

The world says, "Tolerance, evolve, we don't do things like that anymore. This is OK now." But Hebrews 13:8 says Jesus Christ, the same yesterday, today and forever. God does not change His mind.

1 Samuel 15:29 He who is the Glory of Israel does not lie or change his mind; for he is not a man, that he should change his mind."

Numbers 23:19 God is not a man, that he should lie, nor a son of man, that he should change his mind. Does he speak and then not act? Does he promise and not fulfill?

Malachi 3:6 "I the Lord do not change. So you, O descendants of Jacob, are not destroyed."

Psalm 111:10 The fear of the Lord is the beginning of wisdom; all who follow his precepts have good understanding. To him belongs eternal praise.

Remember the fruit of the Holy Spirit: Love, joy, peace, patience, kindness, goodness, faithfulness, gentleness, and self-control? That is Gods Spirit, His personality and character. You want your spirit (your personality and character) and your soul (mind, will and emotions) to be filled with God's Holy Spirit so you can be like Him. When you get saved, God gives you His Holy Spirit (Acts 2:38). Your spirit and God's Holy Spirit communicate with each other. Your soul (mind, will and emotions) begins to change as you learn from God's Holy Spirit by reading the Bible. Your soul is how you are on the inside. How you are on the inside is how you act on the outside. Your spirit (personality and character) is how you act on the outside. Your spirit is what people see. It changes as you feed your soul the Word of God. Your personality and character are a reflection of the Word of God in your mind, will and emotions. It is the Word being put into action. As you <u>choose</u> to do God's Word on the inside (soul), the part people see on the outside (spirit) begins to reflect God's Spirit and His Word, too. This is very powerful. The Holy Spirit cannot bring back to your remembrance when you need it (God's Word), what you have not stored in your mind.

God works from the inside out by filling us with His Holy Spirit. The enemy works from the outside in. That's what he did to Adam and Eve with the fruit. The enemy tries to mess with your spirit (personality and character) on the outside by trying to influence what is on the inside: mind, will and emotions. They all affect the condition of your heart. The enemy cannot get inside of your soul (your mind, will and emotions) without your permission. Never forget that! He absolutely cannot work from the inside out. He has to work from the outside in by setting things in front of your eyes or your ears to damage your soul IF YOU LET HIM. He does this because he doesn't want you to read the Bible or have a relationship with your Heavenly Father. The things you allow in your mouth, eyes and ears affect your spirit and your soul: Word in, Word out, garbage in, garbage out. Don't let the enemy in your soul by way of your mouth, eyes or ears. If something that God tells us is sin is attractive to you, don't set your eyes on it. Don't disobey God by listening to someone or something that will influence you to go in the wrong direction (Luke 10:27).

Luke 10:19 I have given you authority to trample on snakes and scorpions and to overcome all the power of the enemy; nothing will harm you.

I Corinthians 6:18-20 Flee from sexual immorality. All other sins a man commits are outside his body, but he who sins sexually sins against his own body. Do you not know that your body is a temple of the Holy

Spirit, who is in you, whom you have received from God? You are not your own; you were bought at a price. Therefore honor God with your body.

You will notice that the sins the Bible lists that keep us from heaven are sins done to the inside of the body: sexual sins, homosexuality, murder, drunkenness and drugs. The others are internal by way of the heart: liars, magic arts, idolaters, the unbelieving, vile and cowardly. Do they look familiar? These are all issues at the forefront of the world's headlines and that is exactly how you know Satan is involved. He is the greatest liar of all and he's not subtle about it anymore because he knows his time is short: legalization of abortion, gay marriage and drugs, violent entertainment and games that promote sin and death, movies about vampires, the occult, magic spells and the supernatural. All of these things encourage evil and promote Satan's agenda to keep mankind out of heaven. We set them before our children's eyes as entertainment and we buy into the lies of tolerance and choice. We are becoming desensitized to evil. Do you see it? All of these world issues, our entertainment, our attitudes, lifestyles and mindsets are on the lists in the Bible that God warned us would keep us out of heaven. They are a litmus test for the condition of our salvation.

1 Corinthians 6:9-11 Do you not know that the wicked will not inherit the kingdom of God? Do not be deceived: Neither the sexually immoral nor idolaters nor adulterers nor male prostitutes nor homosexual offenders nor thieves nor the greedy nor drunkards nor slanderers nor swindlers will inherit the kingdom of God. And that is what some of you were. But you were washed, you were sanctified, you were justified in the name of the Lord Jesus Christ and by the Spirit of our God.

Galatians 5:19-21 The acts of the sinful nature are obvious: sexual immorality, impurity and debauchery; idolatry and witchcraft; hatred, discord, jealousy, fits of rage, selfish ambition, dissensions, factions and envy; drunkenness, orgies, and the like. I warn you, as I did before, that those who live like this will not inherit the kingdom of God.

Ephesians 5:3-5 But among you there must not be even a hint of sexual immorality, or of any kind of impurity, or of greed, because these are improper for God's holy people. Nor should there be obscenity, foolish talk or coarse joking which are out of place, but rather thanksgiving. For of this you can be sure: No immoral, impure or greedy person – such a man is an idolater – has any inheritance in the kingdom of Christ and of God.

Revelation 21:7-8 He who overcomes will inherit all this, and I will be his God and he will be my son. But the cowardly, the unbelieving, the vile, the murderers, the sexually immoral, those who practice magic arts (drugs), the idolaters and all liars —their place will be in the fiery lake of burning sulfur. This is the second death."

Revelation 22:14-15 "Blessed are those who wash their robes, that they may have the right to the tree of life and may go through the gates into the city. Outside are the dogs, those who practice magic arts, the sexually immoral, the murderers, the idolaters and everyone who loves and practices falsehood.

If we are not very, very careful, we will become polluted by the world.

James 1:27 Religion that God our Father accepts as pure and faultless is this: to look after orphans and widows in their distress and to keep oneself from being polluted by the world.

2 Thessalonians 1:8 He will punish those who do not know God and do not obey the gospel of our Lord Jesus. They will be punished with everlasting destruction and shut out from the presence of the Lord and from the majesty of his power.

Satan does not want you to know how to keep yourself from being polluted by the world or about the lists so he tries to keep us from reading Gods Word. But here is something else he doesn't want you to read about: the cure, the Sword of the Spirit which is praying the Word of God. Prayer is actually talking to God, the Creator of the universe. It is a personal, one on one relationship with the King of Kings and Lord of Lords. Using the scriptures to pray with is the power of God being sent forth to arm His children and disarm the enemies of God. The army of God is a praying army and praying God's Word is our weapon. But only the children of God can be in that praying army. This is a spiritual battle and the choice is yours. You can choose God and His Holy Spirit and Jesus and the cross, or you can choose to join Satan and his evil spirits. Before you decide, you need to know the end of the story.

Revelation 20:10 And the devil, who deceived them, was thrown into the lake of burning sulfur, where the beast and the false prophet had been thrown. They will be tormented day and night for ever and ever.

The battle has already been won, the outcome decided. It wasn't kept a secret. Choose carefully. How important really are the things you want to hold on to? If you choose God's side, you are going to have to change your mind about how you feel about some things. You are going to have to say "no" to the things that Satan has been saying are OK. But don't worry, you are not alone. Your body is a temple of God's Holy Spirit. That means God's Holy Spirit actually takes up residence in you to help you.

John 14:15-17 (Jesus speaking) "If you love me, you will obey what I commanded. And I will ask the Father, and he will give you another Counselor to be with you forever – the Spirit of truth. The world cannot accept him, because it neither sees him nor knows him. But you know him, for he lives with you and will be in you.

John 16:7-11 (Jesus speaking) "But I tell you the truth: It is for your good that I am going away. Unless I go away, the Counselor will not come to you; but if I go, I will send him to you. When he comes, he will convict the world of guilt in regard to sin and righteousness and judgment: in regard to sin, because men do not believe in me; in regard to righteousness because I am going to the Father, where you can see me no longer; and in regard to judgment, because the prince of this world now stands condemned."

But you must be very careful not to grieve the Holy Spirit with your sin. You don't have to understand, you just have to make the choice to obey in faith. As you choose to obey, you begin to understand. Understanding does not always come first.

Ephesians 4:30 And do not grieve the Holy Spirit of God, with whom you were sealed for the day of redemption.

"Well," you say, "God knows we are weak and He knows our hearts and that we really mean well. We are doing this in love, it's just a game, it's pretend, it's not a child yet, it's legal, I don't do it often, it's not an idol, it's a decoration. We didn't know and He will forgive us anyway because He is a loving God and I asked Jesus into my heart. Besides, the Bible was written a long time ago and times have changed and this is OK now."

Ephesians 4:17-24 So I tell you this, and insist on it in the Lord, that you must no longer live as the Gentiles do, in the futility of their thinking. They are darkened in their understanding and separated from the life of God because of the ignorance that is in them due to the hardening of their hearts. Having lost all sensitivity, they have given themselves over to sensuality so as to indulge in every kind of impurity, and they are full of greed. That, however, is not the way of life you learned when you heard about Christ and were taught in him in accordance with the truth that is in Jesus. You were taught, with regard to your former way of life, to put off your old self, which is being corrupted by its deceitful desires; to be made new in the attitude of your minds; and to put on the new self, created to be like God in true righteousness and holiness.

198

Psalm 119:11 (KJV) Thy word have I hid in mine heart, that I might not sin against thee.

If you have God's words hidden in your heart, you will recognize the lies of the world. The world teaches tolerance, worldly love and a modern evolved church that revolves around the political correctness of their understanding about how God should work. Everyone wants there to be a "god" but the problem is that they want their "god" to agree with their point of view. The world's "gods" just have to be tolerant of their way of thinking. But God's love is very different from the world's love and the world does not understand. Your time here on earth is short, but eternity is a very long time so you need to study and understand the living God, the eternal God.

God is not mean. God knows how evil the enemy is. He knows all the enemy's tricks. That's why God tells us to obey His Word and listen to His Son Jesus. He loves you and gave you everything you needed for salvation and joy, but you listened to the world instead and went your own way because the world gives you permission to sin and says you will be saved anyway. You believed a lie even though God told you the truth. Others told you the truth: Pastors, your family, TV ministers, books, billboards, songs, friends, strangers, even angels in disguise. But you did your own thing. Don't be mad at God. You lost your salvation all by yourself. You looked, said yes and jumped.

Get wisdom so you can fear the Lord. Read your Bible so you will learn how God wants you to live. Let God breathe on you through His Word. If you want understanding, follow His precepts. Make sure you belong to God.

John 8:47 "He who belongs to God hears what God says. The reason you do not hear is that you do not belong to God."

Proverbs 5:21-23 For a man's ways are in full view of the Lord, and he examines all his paths. The evil deeds of a wicked man ensnare him;

the cords of his sin hold him fast. He will die for lack of discipline, led astray by his own great folly.

Isaiah 55:8 "For my thoughts are not your thoughts, neither are your ways my ways," declares the Lord.

Your spirit must be born again. That is what died in the Garden of Eden. Your mind, will and emotions (soul) must learn to line up with God's way of thinking, not your own. That is a wonderful, wonderful plan. We get a second chance. We have to be born again and change our way of thinking and living to His. He loves us so much, He sacrificed His own Son so we could live with Him forever. God made a way for us through the blood of Jesus to come boldly to Him without condemnation, guilt or shame. When we accept the blood, we are cleansed and we can go to heaven without sin in us because God sees the blood of His Son instead of our sin. He sees our new, born again nature. When you are born again, you are a changed person. You cannot go to heaven as the same person you were. No matter how good or bad you are, you must be born again. We must live to please God, not ourselves.

2 Peter 2:4-10 For if God did not spare angels when they sinned, but sent them to hell, putting them into gloomy dungeons to be held for judgment; if he did not spare the ancient world when he brought the flood on its ungodly people, but protected Noah, a preacher of righteousness, and seven others; If he condemned the cities of Sodom and Gomorrah by burning them to ashes, and made them an example of what is going to happen to the ungodly; and if he rescued Lot, a righteous man, who was distressed by the filthy lives of lawless men (for that righteous man, living among them day after day, was tormented in his righteous soul by the lawless deeds he saw and heard) – if this is so, then the Lord knows how to rescue godly men from trials and to hold the unrighteous for the day of judgment, while continuing their punishment. This is especially true of those who follow the corrupt desire of the sinful nature and despise authority.

200

Matthew 13:40-43 "As the weeds are pulled up and burned in the fire, so it will be at the end of the age. The Son of Man will send out his angels, and they will weed out of his kingdom everything that causes sin and all who do evil. They will throw them into the fiery furnace, where there will be weeping and gnashing of teeth. Then the righteous will shine like the sun in the kingdom of their Father. He who has ears, let him hear."

Psalm 97:10 Let those who love the Lord hate evil, for he guards the lives of his faithful ones and delivers them from the hand of the wicked.

The tree of the knowledge of good and evil had purpose. We have been given the opportunity to choose again. When you know the choice and the truth, good is so very great and evil is so very small. Man is not automatically saved because he is "man" and he is not automatically saved because he believes in God. Make your choice, and then live it. Heaven is ready. He who has ears let him hear.

Hebrews 9:27-28 Just as man is destined to die once, and after that to face judgment, so Christ was sacrificed once to take away the sins of many people; and he will appear a second time, not to bear sin, but to bring salvation to those who are waiting for him.

1 Corinthians 1:18 For the message of the cross is foolishness to those who are perishing, but to us who are being saved it is the power of God.

Romans 6:1-2 What shall we say, then? Shall we go on sinning so that grace may increase? By no means! We died to sin; how can we live in it any longer?

This is a spiritual battle not a flesh and blood battle. Our mighty God is in control and His Son Jesus has already conquered the enemy; it is finished. The history of the world was revealed to us in the garden and recorded for us in the Bible, and it all started with one little lie.

Chapter 9
WHEN THE ARMY OF GOD SINS

Psalm 1:1-2
Blessed is the man who does not walk in the counsel of the wicked or
stand in the way of sinners or sit in the seat of mockers. But his delight
is in the law of the Lord and on his law he meditates day and night.

Perhaps one of the best illustrations in the Bible of the consequences of sin is Jericho. Moses died and now Joshua is in charge. The Israelites have been wandering 40 years because of their rebellion and unbelief. Now they are finally going to enter the promised land. God told Joshua that He would give him every place where he sets his foot and to be strong and courageous and He would never fail or forsake him.

God also gave Joshua the instructions for prosperity and good success. Not just success, but "good" success. He was to read the Book of the Law day and night and do what it says. He could not let it depart from his mouth. That means Joshua was to speak the Book of the Law day and night. That way he would remember to do everything in it exactly the way God told him. That was the key to their success. The Bible is our book of the law. It tells us how to live saved and have good success. Just like Joshua our victories will not be without the price of obedience. As it was with Adam and Eve, Abraham, Isaac, Jacob and Moses, God promises abundant life, prosperity and success, yet they are conditional upon obeying God. It boils down to one word: sin. It has the power to ruin everything, so don't do it.

Joshua 1:1-9 (KJV) Now after the death of Moses the servant of the Lord, the Lord spake to Joshua son of Nun, Moses' minister, saying, "Moses my servant is dead; now therefore arise, go over this Jordan, thou, and all this people, unto the land which I do give to them, even to the children of Israel. Every place that the sole of your foot shall tread upon, that have I given unto you, as I said unto Moses. From the wilderness and this Lebanon even unto the great river Euphrates, all the land of the Hittites, and unto the Great Sea toward the going down of the sun, shall be your coast. There shall not any man be able to stand before thee all the days of thy life: as I was with Moses, so I will be with thee: I will not fail thee, nor forsake thee. Be strong and of a good courage: for unto this people shalt thou divide for an inheritance the land, which I sware unto their fathers to give them. Only be thou strong and very courageous, that thou mayest observe to do according to all the law, which Moses my servant commanded thee: turn not from it to the right hand or to the left, that thou mayest prosper withersoever thou goest. This book of the law shall not depart out of thy mouth; but thou shalt meditate therein day and night, that thou mayest observe to do according to all that is written therein: for then thou shalt make thy way prosperous, and then thou shalt have good success. Have not I commanded thee? Be strong and of a good courage; be not afraid, neither be thou dismayed: for the Lord thy God is with thee whithersoever thou goest."

We have to pause here and take notice. When God tells you three times in a row to be strong and courageous and don't be afraid or dismayed because He will be with you, it means something is coming that is going to give you the opportunity to be weak, without courage, afraid and dismayed. When He says it three times in the same instruction, and adds the word "very" to courageous, you had better have your eyes and ears wide open!

This is an exciting time in the life of the Israelites. God told Joshua to get ready. They are finally receiving the promised inheritance of their forefathers. They have been waiting for forty years and 430 years before that. Now it is time to get ready. In three days they will cross the Jordan River and take possession of the land. No doubt before the parents died, they told their children the stories of how they were delivered from Egyptian bondage and how God parted the waters for them. They told them the stories of Abraham and the Promised Land and now it is time for the children to receive the inheritance. The children have seen their own rebellion and deliverances along the way. They followed the same cloud and pillar of fire and now they get to see God part the waters of the Jordan River for them as He had the Red Sea for their parents. God is building their faith and showing them His great love. He is exalting Joshua in their eyes so they will know that God is with him as He was with Moses.

They get circumcised at Gilgal and celebrate the Passover for the first time since Mt. Sinai. The manna has stopped and now they are ready to take the inheritance of Canaan and the first city is Jericho. This time Joshua secretly sends in two spies. They are encouraged by Rahab's report of fear and they give Joshua a good report.

So Joshua and the Israelites go in and take Jericho. But before they went in, just like Moses before him, Joshua tells the people what to do with all the Jericho "stuff." They are not to take anything for themselves, nothing. No souvenirs this time.

Joshua 6:17-19 The city and all that is in it are to be devoted to the Lord. Only Rahab the prostitute and all who are with her in her house shall be spared, because she hid the spies we sent. But keep away from the devoted things, so that you will not bring about your own destruction by taking any of them. Otherwise you will make the camp of

Israel liable to destruction and bring trouble on it. All the silver and gold and the articles of bronze and Iron are sacred to the Lord and must go into his treasury."

Jericho was the first city of the inheritance to be taken. Think of the tithe here. Your tithe is the first fruit of your paycheck. It is set-aside for God because it belongs to Him and therefore it is sacred. That means it is holy, consecrated, set apart for God. Jericho is the first of the cities of Canaan to be taken and, therefore, is the first tithe of the Promised Land. But it is also a "first fruit." The tithe is one tenth, but the first fruit is the whole thing. The whole city of Jericho is a first fruit, holy to the Lord. It represented a first of all the cities that God was giving them. It is a city that was set apart, dedicated and completely given to God. The "stuff" in it is set-apart, devoted to God. The devoted things, the things that were dedicated to God, could not be touched. All the metals; silver, gold, bronze and iron were saved for God's treasury as God had instructed them. Everything else was destroyed with the sword and then burned with fire. The King James Version calls the devoted things, "accursed." There is a curse attached to the devoted things so that when you take them, the curse attaches itself to you. Just like idols and sin.

Joshua 6:18 (KJV) And ye, in any wise keep yourselves from the accursed thing, lest ye make yourselves accursed, when ye take of the accursed thing, and make the camp of Israel a curse, and trouble it.

Now it is the seventh day. Forty years of wandering have come down to this moment. Wouldn't you love to have been there? Israel is finally entering the Promised Land. There is silence while they listen to Joshua give the final instructions. Joshua tells the people not to take the devoted things or they will "make the camp of Israel liable to destruction and bring trouble on it." They have already marched around the city the seventh time. God told the people that on the seventh day, after the seventh time around the city, when they hear the long blast on the

206

trumpet, they are to shout. Then, of all things, the wall is going to collapse. Who does that? Can you imagine? Israel couldn't wait to see it! They were on pins and needles waiting to shout. Can you imagine watching all of this from the other side of the wall? Jericho probably thought they were nuts! Rahab said they were terrified. Israel's reputation had gone before them. Now Israel is being told that the whole camp would be legally responsible for its own destruction if they take anything. Prepare your hearts, eyes and minds before you go in so you will deal correctly with the stuff. It was already out there. Destruction would be the price for liability. You will be destroyed. Not just you but the whole camp. How did Achan miss that?

Now it's time! The trumpet sounded a long blast and finally the people shouted. This was no little shout. This shout was more than two million people releasing 40 years of wandering frustration. It was the obedient shout of something new in the air: home at last, the fulfillment of a long awaited promise. What did they say when they shouted? Was it praise and worship? Was it thanksgiving or just noise? How long did the shouting last? It must have been deafening. And then, wonder of wonders, the walls fell down and the feet of the Israelites touched home for the first time, absolutely incredible. What a beginning into the promise.

Really they did pretty well considering how many there were. Everything went according to plan and they took Jericho. There were at least forty thousand fighting men who went in (Joshua 4:13). That is a lot of people! Out of the forty thousand, thirty-nine thousand, nine hundred and ninety nine obeyed God and Joshua. What are the odds of that? It is absolutely incredible that that many people obeyed. Only one man blew it, one man! But God wasn't looking for a job "pretty well" done. He needed complete obedience. Israel doesn't know about the "one man" and God told them that it is time to go into the promised land, so now that Jericho has been taken, they are moving on to the next city. The Bible doesn't say that they consulted with God first.

That would be another lesson learned. So Joshua sent three thousand men to take the city of Ai.

It was a disaster. There were only a few men in Ai, so it should have been easy. Instead, the men of Ai routed the army of Israel. That means Israel retreated and ran away. Thirty-six of them are killed and this time, it is the hearts of Israel that melt and become like water (Joshua 7:5). What happened?

Joshua and all Israel, except maybe the "one" are shocked. Everything has stopped. Joshua is on his face before the Ark of the Lord with torn clothes until evening. The elders of Israel did the same thing. All of Israel has completely stopped. There is no tomorrow, only the here and now. In their minds, entrance to the promised land has stopped. Going forward has stopped. The reputation of Israel and their God is in jeopardy. Their minds are consumed with the fear that is trying to store itself in their hearts. Then the Lord speaks to Joshua.

Joshua 7:10 The Lord said to Joshua, "Stand up! What are you doing down on your face?"

Why don't we listen to God? Joshua did not belong on his face. He belonged in the camp. He should have been going through the camp looking for the person responsible. This is what God was talking about when He told Joshua to be strong and have courage and obey the law. What happened was exactly what God said would happen if they sinned.

Joshua 6:18 But keep away from the devoted things, so that you will not bring about your own destruction by taking any of them. Otherwise you will make the camp of Israel liable to destruction and bring trouble on it.

That is exactly what happened. Let's read the rest:

Joshua 7:10-12 The Lord said to Joshua, "Stand up! What are you doing down on your face? Israel has sinned; they have violated my

208

covenant, which I commanded them to keep. They have taken some of the devoted things; they have stolen, they have lied, they have put them with their own possessions. That is why the Israelites cannot stand against their enemies; they turn their backs and run because they have been made liable to destruction. I will not be with you anymore unless you destroy whatever among you is devoted to destruction."

The scariest part is the first part of the last sentence: "I will not be with you anymore " It is cut and dried. It is the last straw. This sounds like a contradiction because God told Joshua He would never leave him or forsake him. But God's covenant (contract) that God had "commanded them to keep" had been violated. It was based on complete obedience and it had been broken by Israel. But in His infinite, never ceasing mercy, God offers an "unless." It is a way out. Notice God does not say only one man sinned. He said "Israel" has sinned. "They" have violated. "They" have taken. "They" have stolen. "They" have lied. "They" put the devoted things (God's stuff) with their own possessions. That is why they cannot stand against their enemies. "They" have been made liable. Israel is a unified group. They count as one. If you are with a group of people who do wrong, you get in trouble, too, because you are with them. Now all of Israel is in trouble because of the "one." God will not be with them anymore unless they "destroy whatever among them is devoted to destruction." It is an obedience issue, a yeast issue and a holiness issue. They have to obey God to get the blessings. They have to watch each other and keep each other from sin because the sin of just one would spread like yeast in the camp. God cannot be in the presence of sin. So God said "Stand up!" In others words, fix it quickly so we can move on.

Let's pause here and dissect "liable to destruction." Liable means to be legally responsible. When you are liable in a court of law, you are the legally responsible party. In other words, it is your fault; it happened because of you. Therefore, your actions are subject to a legal re-action. Not only are you legally responsible, but there will also be legal action for or against you. In a court of law, you have to wait for your penalty. In this case God warned them in the same sentence what the penalty would be: destruction.

Notice that the last verse changes from "made liable to destruction" to "devoted to destruction." Devoted means "dedicated." It has been earmarked for a purpose. All of the stuff in Jericho had been dedicated to God and therefore it was to be destroyed as a sacrifice. Israel had become legally responsible for their own destruction because they had in their possession "something" that was supposed to be devoted to destruction as a first fruit for God. Only the metals were supposed to be saved because they were sacred (holy, set apart) to the Lord for His treasury. So something was stolen that belonged to God's treasury or should have been destroyed or both. But there is a second meaning to "devoted to destruction." It can also be applied to a person being devoted or committed to destruction by their actions.

In Israel's case, the consequence had been named before the crime. Everyone already knew what would happen if they took anything for themselves. Joshua was so careful to warn them about the devoted things. Right after they marched around Jericho on the seventh day, for the seventh time, just before the last trumpet blast, Joshua gave them the instructions and the warning. Then the trumpets blew, the people shouted, the walls fell down and every man charged straight in and took the city! If thirty-nine thousand, nine hundred and ninety nine men heard the warning, Achan did too. Now the whole camp is in trouble and Achan is responsible for God's anger, Israel's failure, and the deaths of 36 innocent men who had obeyed.

The covenant with God was that if Israel obeyed Him, He would be with them. That has been broken by Israel. Repentance needs to take place to move on. That can only be done if the accursed is removed. God gave instructions for "the accursed" and the "accursed thing." The accursed "thing" had to be taken

210

away outside the camp with the "accursed" and be destroyed. In other words, get rid of the thing and destroy the person who is legally responsible. God said Israel was doomed to destruction. Doomed is not a good thing. There is no good way out of doomed.

Now God tells the people to sanctify themselves. That meant to wash their clothes and purify themselves to get ready to meet with God the next day. There was going to be judgment in the sight of all the people.

Joshua 7:13-15 "Go, consecrate the people. Tell them, 'consecrate yourselves in preparation for tomorrow; for this is what the Lord, the God of Israel, says: That which is devoted is among you, O Israel. You cannot stand against your enemies until you remove it. In the morning, present yourselves tribe by tribe. The tribe that the Lord takes shall come forward clan by clan; the clan that the Lord takes shall come forward family by family; and the family that the Lord takes shall come forward man by man. He who is caught with the devoted things shall be destroyed by fire, along with all that belongs to him. He has violated the covenant of the Lord and has done a disgraceful thing in Israel!'"

Joshua has to tell the people whoever is caught with the devoted things has to be destroyed by fire along with all that belongs to him. Everyone must have been asking each other "Did you?" Frantic mothers and fathers would be searching their tents to see if it was their family at fault. Can you imagine how it would feel to be Achan? Can you imagine the horror Achan must have felt after hearing that? He could not have slept at all that night knowing what was going to happen to him and his family. Why didn't he run away or why didn't he just confess then? It was obvious that God knew what he had done. Maybe he still thought he wouldn't be found out. Why, after all God had done for them? That is arrogance, unbelief in that he didn't believe he would get caught, greed and rebellion against God. The consequences of his sin would fall on the whole camp. It was a lesson their parents had already gone through and now they would learn it for themselves.

Early the next morning Israel presented themselves to Joshua by tribes, clans, families and man by man. There were sighs of relief as tribes and clans were passed by and finally, sadly, the family of Achan was chosen and Achan was taken. There was dead silence while Achan confessed.

Joshua 7:19 Then Joshua said to Achan, "My son, give glory to the Lord, the God of Israel, and honor him. Tell me what you have done; do not hide it from me."

Joshua 7:20 Achan replied, "It is true! I have sinned against the Lord, the God of Israel. This is what I have done: When I saw in the plunder a beautiful robe from Babylonia, two hundred shekels of silver and a wedge of gold weighing fifty shekels, I coveted them and took them. They are hidden in the ground inside my tent, with the silver underneath."

(Psalm 36:1-4 An oracle is within my heart concerning the sinfulness of the wicked: There is no fear of God before his eyes. For in his own eyes he flatters himself too much to detect or hate his sin. The words of his mouth are wicked and deceitful; he has ceased to be wise and to do good. Even on his bed he plots evil; he commits himself to a sinful course and does not reject what is wrong.)

He did not turn his eyes away from temptation. Achan feasted his eyes on the things devoted to God. He allowed covetousness, pride, greed and lust to settle in his heart because he did not prepare his heart and eyes before he went in. He did not love God, Israel or his family more than a robe, gold or silver. He knew what he did was wrong because he hid it! That means he did know the consequences. He did hear what God told Joshua to tell the people. Then he waited until he absolutely had to before he confessed. Maybe he was hoping someone else would get blamed. He was still trying to get away with it even until the last minute. Then he attempted to get out of the situation by confessing. But did you notice that there was no repentance? He never said, "I'm sorry, I will never do it again." The consequences were absolute so he would not get out of the punishment, but we see his heart condition very clearly here. What a lesson for all of Israel. What a terrible, terrible day for everyone. Joshua sent messengers to go and get the devoted things and they spread them out before the Lord. By doing so, the sin was exposed. That is the beginning of cleansing.

Can you imagine the utter horror of the moment for everyone? Especially the family of Achan. The things he took were so small, but it was no little thing that Achan did. He stole from God. He was responsible for the thirty-six men who died innocently and were robbed of living in the Promised Land and for the agony of their families that were left behind. He was responsible for the impending death of his own family. He was responsible for the reputation of Israel and her God when Israel was routed by Ai. All of this for a robe and a little bit of silver and gold. Now, not only are the things he stole accursed (doomed), but everything that belongs to him has become infected and is also accursed. Everything related to Achan is doomed, his family and even his tent. There would be no plunder from the tent of Achan. His confession would not save him or his family, but it would save Israel.

Joshua 7:24-26 Then Joshua, together with all Israel, took Achan son of Zerah, the silver, the robe, the gold wedge, his sons and daughters, his cattle, donkeys and sheep, his tent and all that he had, to the Valley of Achor. Joshua said, "Why have you brought this trouble on us? The Lord will bring trouble on you today." Then all Israel stoned him, and after they had stoned the rest, they burned them. Over Achan they heaped up a large pile of rocks, which remains to this day. Then the Lord turned from his fierce anger. Therefore that place has been called the Valley of Achor ever since.

Can you imagine having to pick up a stone and be a part of that dreadful day? Do you see the parallel between Rahab and Achan? Rahab's family and all that belonged to her were saved from destruction because of her faith in Israel's God. They were saved because of the faith of the one. Achan and his family and all who belonged to him were destroyed for the disobedience of the one. Deuteronomy tells us why. Moses had to deal with the same thing.

Deuteronomy 19:20 The rest of the people will hear of this and be afraid, and never again will such an evil thing be done among you.

Sin is evil in every way. Now that the sin has been dealt with, the blessing of Ai that has been on hold can be released. God told Joshua to take the whole army and attack Ai just like they did at Jericho, only this time the plunder is theirs to keep. So God delivered Ai into Israel's hands.

God is not terrible. It is our willingness to sin that is terrible. We are Achan. Right now, the significance of the blood of Jesus should be ringing loud and clear to you. If the blood of Jesus had been available to Achan, he would not have died for his sin if he had repented. The blood of Jesus would have covered it, but Achan would still have to repent and get rid of the stuff. God was preparing His people, Israel, to be a nation for Himself. God's own Son would be born from this people and be tortured and killed for the sins of the whole world. Israel was promised everything good for her obedience. She was warned about disobedience. It may not seem fair at the moment, but it is never just about the moment. God, who is perfect and omnipresent, the Ancient of Days, is our loving Father. He orchestrates events for our salvation. Everything we are about points to heaven. We cannot live how we want to in any old way while we are here on the earth. It doesn't matter if you agree with God or not. It is obedience or destruction. The destruction of Achan in your life is paramount to your moving on with God. Your whole life is on hold until you deal with your sin. It starts out with salvation, but that is just the beginning. Now you have to be obedient. Achan believed in God. He ate manna and saw the waters part. He was a believer who died because of his willful, deliberate, presumptuous, unrepentant sin and took those attached to him with him. He didn't believe he would get caught or that God would really carry out the sentence. How many "Christians" today believe the same thing about their sin.

Numbers 15:30-31 But anyone who sins defiantly, whether native-born or alien, blasphemes the Lord, and that person must be cut off from his people. Because he has despised the Lord's word and broken his commands, that person must surely be cut off; his guilt remains on him.

Deuteronomy 17:12 (KJV) And the man that will do presumptuously, and will not hearken unto the priest that standeth to minister there before the Lord thy God, or unto the judge, even that man shall die: and thou shalt put away the evil from Israel.

Psalm 19:13 Keep your servant also from willful sins; may they not rule over me. Then will I be blameless, innocent of great transgressions.

2 Peter 2:10 This is especially true of those who follow the corrupt desire of the sinful nature and despise authority.

Presumptuous sin is when you sin willingly, on purpose knowing that God said not to do it. You commit willful sins because you want your own way and you think God will forgive you anyway when you repent. The Bible says presumptuous sin is defiant and evil. It blasphemes the Lord. It is a great transgression and by doing it, you despise authority. This is a heart condition. You need to check what you have stored in your heart.

Luke 13:22-30 Then Jesus went through the towns and villages, teaching as he made his way to Jerusalem. Someone asked him, "Lord, are only a few people going to be saved?" He said to them, "Make every

215

effort to enter through the narrow door, because many, I tell you, will try
to enter and will not be able to. Once the owner of the house gets up and
closes the door, you will stand outside knocking and pleading, 'Sir, open
the door for us.' "But he will answer, 'I don't know you or where you
come from.' "Then you will say, 'We ate and drank with you, and you
taught in our streets.' "But he will reply, 'I don't know you or where
you come from. Away from me, all you evildoers!' "There will be
weeping there, and gnashing of teeth, when you see Abraham, Isaac and
Jacob and all the prophets in the kingdom of God, but you yourselves
thrown out. People will come from east and west and north and south,
and will take their places at the feast in the kingdom of God. Indeed there
are those who are last who will be first, and first who will be last."

Because of the blood of Jesus you don't have to die for the plunder in your tent. But you do have to repent and get rid of it. If you don't, you will die, too. Achan did not have the luxury of repentance that day. We do. The sins in your tent are no less accursed just because Jesus died. The sin in your life is no less accursed just because you are a believer. The sin is doomed and you are, too, just like Achan's family if you don't separate yourself from it. You cannot enter heaven attached to sin. If that were true, the death of Jesus on the cross was for nothing, a waste of time and a lie. Achan didn't die because he didn't believe in God. He died because he didn't obey, and his household perished with him.

Sin is very, very expensive. It cost God his only son Jesus on the cross. It cost the angels their home in heaven and separation from God. It cost Adam and Eve their home in Eden and separation from God and brought sin into the world. It cost Israel their home and separation from God, and it costs us our home in heaven and separation from God for all eternity.

We cannot talk about sin without bringing grace into the picture. Grace is freedom from sin. It is God's kindness towards us. Grace is when you get from God what you don't deserve. It offers a way out of sin, but it is not always available to us in the way we would like. The grace of God as a way out of sin by animal sacrifice did not apply to Achan and Israel on this day in this situation. It did on other days, but not this one. God did not offer a way out if they sinned when they went into Jericho. No sacrifices, repentance, offerings, nothing but destruction. Justice is when you get what you deserve. Justice would be the fair price for failure that day. The grace of God was in the verbal warning. God made it very clear that complete obedience was required. It was easy. Don't take anything. If you do, you will be destroyed. It was an obedience day. The grace was in the warning not in the way out.

We can trace the verbal warnings of God's grace all the way back to Adam and Eve in the garden when God told them not to eat the fruit or else. We see it in the conversation between God and Cain about mastering sin before Cain killed Abel. We see the verbal warnings in the lives of Abraham, Isaac, Jacob, Joseph, Moses, Joshua, the judges, priests, kings and the prophets. The entire New Testament is a verbal warning for us to stay far away from sin.

Matthew 7:21-23 "Not everyone who says to me, 'Lord, Lord,' will enter the kingdom of heaven, but only the one who does the will of my Father who is in heaven. Many will say to me on that day, 'Lord, Lord, did we not prophesy in your name and in your name drive out demons and in your name perform many miracles?' Then I will tell them plainly, 'I never knew you. Away from me, you evildoers!'"

The death of Jesus on the cross, made available to us a whole new grace. It did not negate the former verbal grace, but rather it enhanced it. It gave us a way out of sin, but it is not a get out of sin free card. It is not a license to sin freely. Jesus said only the one who does the will of his Father will enter the kingdom. Those are your "deeds" after you are saved.

James 1:25 But the man who looks intently into the perfect law that gives freedom, and continues to do this, not forgetting what he has heard, but doing it – he will be blessed in what he does.

James 2:14-26 What good is it, my brothers, if a man claims to have faith but has no deeds? Can such faith save him? Suppose a brother or sister is without clothes and daily food. If one of you says to him, "Go, I wish you well; keep warm and well fed," but does nothing about his physical needs, what good is it? In the same way, faith by itself, if it is not accompanied by action, is dead.

But someone will say, "You have faith; I have deeds."

Show me your faith without deeds, and I will show you my faith by what I do. You believe that there is one God. Good! Even the demons believe that—and shudder.

You foolish man, do you want evidence that faith without deeds is useless? Was not our ancestor Abraham considered righteous for what he did when he offered his son Isaac on the altar? You see that his faith and his actions were working together, and his faith was made complete by what he did. And the scripture was fulfilled that says, "Abraham believed God, and it was credited to him as righteousness," and he was called God's friend. You see that a person is justified by what he does and not by faith alone.

In the same way, was not even Rahab the prostitute considered righteous for what she did when she gave lodging to the spies and sent them off in a different direction? As the body without the spirit is dead, so faith without deeds is dead.

James 3:13 Who is wise and understanding among you? Let him show it by his good life, by deeds done in the humility that comes from wisdom.

A license is a permit with guidelines. It gives opportunity and freedom to do something. You need permits to build walls in your yard. You need permits to build buildings, have businesses, go fishing, drive, and practice law or medicine. You have to apply for and pay a fee for a permit or license that gives you permission to do something that requires it. You then have the freedom to exercise your permit within the required guidelines. That means you have to obey the laws of the permit. If you have a permit to build a wall that is six feet high and you decide to go ten feet, you need a new permit. If you disobey, the law allows punishment. The wall has to come down, you are fined, your business is closed or you lose your permit etc.

Now listen carefully. The grace of God is a license. But it is not a license to sin freely. The grace of God is a license to repent.

Grace (the loving kindness of God) does not excuse repentance. Grace expects repentance and waits patiently for it. The kindness (grace) of God does not mean it is ok to keep sinning now that you are saved. Grace is always there for you but its benefits (salvation, sanctification, redemption, justification, forgiveness, blessings and holiness etc.) are activated in your life by your repentance. God's grace brings you to salvation but the benefits of God's grace come after salvation. Repentance means you changed your mind about the sins you were committing and decided to believe what God says in His Word and follow Jesus. Repentance says I'm sorry and I'm not doing that anymore. Grace says "I love you and I forgive you now let's move on." Grace is how God feels about you and repentance is how you feel about God. Grace is God's gift to you and repentance is your gift to God.

And yet our salvation is not by works. We cannot earn our way to heaven. The gift of salvation is free. But there is a big difference between <u>doing good</u> things to <u>earn</u> your salvation verses <u>being obedient</u> because you <u>are</u> saved. The bible makes it very clear that life of the saved man is different and that because you are saved, you make changes in your life that reflect holiness. God tells us in His Word to be holy because He is holy. He wants us to match Him not the world. Just like Israel, we are sanctified (set apart, different from the world, and made holy) and justified (just as if I'd never done it) because of the blood of Jesus.

Un-repentance stalls your walk with God. It puts His agenda for your life on hold until you come back to Him. Grace and mercy are always there waiting for you as you grow in holiness. Holiness is a choice. How you live your life is your testimony to the world and also to God. He knows those who are His.

2 Timothy 2:19 Nevertheless, God's solid foundation stands firm, sealed with this inscription: "The Lord knows those who are his," and, "Everyone who confesses the name of the Lord must turn away from wickedness."

Deuteronomy 7:9 Know therefore that the Lord your God is God; he is the faithful God, keeping his covenant of love to a thousand generations of those who love him and keep his commandments.

Grace is the opportunity to repent and be saved no matter what you've done. Grace is available to you before and after salvation. It gives you permission to come before the throne of God because you became a part of His family through your salvation. It requires action on your part. God is not going to magically sprinkle salvation down from heaven and whoever it lands on gets saved. The action of the application is your asking for salvation. You have to ask for it. The answer is always "yes!" God will not just dump salvation on you without your permission. There is love in both the asking and the giving. There is no fee for your salvation because Jesus paid the price. The whole point of salvation is to have the opportunity to live forever in heaven with God instead of going to hell. The benefit of salvation is to have God on your side here on earth to help you out. You get all the benefits of God's inheritance without actually having to die a physical death first. He is your Abba Father, your daddy. We don't deserve salvation because of our sins, but grace says it doesn't matter what you did before, your salvation is a free gift. Everyone can be saved through faith. You do not have to qualify for the free license of Grace. Your sin qualifies you. Grace is unmerited, undeserved favor.

Before Jesus shed His blood, only the High Priest could go behind the curtain and be in the presence of God and only once a year.

Leviticus 16:2 The Lord said to Moses: "Tell your brother Aaron not to come whenever he chooses into the Most Holy Place behind the curtain in front of the atonement cover on the ark, or else he will die, because I appear in the cloud over the atonement cover.

Leviticus 16:34 "This is to be a lasting ordinance for you: Atonement is to be made once a year for all the sins of the Israelites." And it was done, as the Lord commanded Moses.

Leviticus 16:13 He is to put the incense on the fire before the Lord, and the smoke of the incense will conceal the atonement cover above the Testimony, so that he will not die.

Remember, God cannot be in the presence of sin. We cannot be in the presence of God in our sinful condition or we will die. The heavy curtain separated man from the presence of God. The smoke of the incense would separate the priest and God from viewing each other. In order for the priest to go behind the curtain, he had to wear special clothes, bathe, offer sacrifices for his own sin and the sin of his family. He had to be completely clean. There was a lot to do and it took all day. Everything had to be perfect for him to enter the presence of God and still he had to hide behind the smoke. Then the priest would take a bowl of sacrificial animal blood and sprinkle it on the atonement cover of the Ark for the sins of the people, but it was a temporary fix. It had to be repeated every year because it wasn't enough.

Now listen! That curtain that separated man from the presence of God in the Holy of Holies was ripped in two from the top to the bottom at the moment Jesus died. We don't need the curtain, the smoke of incense to hide us, the priest as a mediator or the sacrificial blood of goats and lambs anymore. Jesus is the sacrificial Lamb of God and our High Priest. His blood is the last

221

sacrifice. His blood is the curtain and the smoke of incense that makes us clean and completely covers us and our sins, head to toe forever so we can actually be in the presence of God ourselves. We can ask God anything in Jesus name because Jesus is our mediator. When you get saved, you are covered by His blood. The blood of Jesus was enough and it lasts forever and ever.

Isaiah 1:18 "Come now, let us reason together," says the Lord. "Though your sins are like scarlet, they shall be as white as snow; though they are red as crimson, they shall be like wool.

Hebrews 6:19 We have this hope as an anchor for the soul, firm and secure. It enters the inner sanctuary behind the curtain, where Jesus, who went before us, has entered on our behalf. He has become a high priest forever, in the order of Melchizedek.

Hebrews 7:27 Unlike the other high priests, he does not need to offer sacrifices day after day, first for his own sins, and then for the sins of the people. He sacrificed for their sins once for all when he offered himself.

Hebrews 9:12-14 He did not enter by means of the blood of goats and calves; but he entered the Most Holy Place once for all by his own blood, having obtained eternal redemption. The blood of goats and bulls and the ashes of a heifer sprinkled on those who are ceremonially unclean sanctify them so that they are outwardly clean. How much more, then, will the blood of Christ, who through the eternal Spirit offered himself unblemished to God, cleanse our consciences from acts that lead to death, so that we may serve the living God!

The grace of God allowed His only Son to die so God could be with us. The blood of Jesus is how much God loves us. It is how mankind is able to live in heaven with God forever. It was God's plan from the very beginning.

2 Timothy 1:9-10 He has saved us and called us to a holy life—not because of anything we have done but because of his own purpose and grace. This grace was given us in Christ Jesus before the beginning of time, but it has now been revealed through the appearing of our Savior, Christ Jesus, who has destroyed death and has brought life and immortality to light through the gospel.

John 19:30 When he had received the drink, Jesus said, "It is finished." With that, he bowed his head and gave up his spirit.

Ephesians 3:11-12 according to his eternal purpose which he accomplished in Christ Jesus our Lord. In him and through faith in him we may approach God with freedom and confidence.

We cannot be in the presence of God without the blood of Jesus covering our sins. That is the story of the Bible. That is what salvation is. That is what the Gospel message is all about. That is what the Old Testament points us to and what the New Testament delivers. The blood of Jesus is why there is a nation of Israel. The blood of Jesus is why we can live in heaven forever with God. But you can't be in the family of God if you reject the blood of Jesus. The only thing that can save you is faith in the atoning blood of Jesus Christ. When you have that faith, the way you live your life will prove it.

The license of your salvation gives you the freedom and opportunity (grace) to come before God and repent of your sins because you are covered by the blood of the Lamb. Now we can ask God for ourselves and have our own relationship with God and Jesus and the Holy Spirit. We enter the Holy of Holies with worship and a sacrifice of praise and thanksgiving. The blood of Jesus is your permit to come before the throne of God and be in His presence and receive His grace for your life. Grace is a license to repent after you have blown it as a Christian and say, "Whoops! I'm sorry I did that God. I won't do it anymore. Thank you for forgiving me. Please show me how to fix this." God's mercy is very patient. Grace is when you get what you don't deserve and mercy is when you don't get what you deserve. He will always forgive a repentant sinner.

Hebrews 4:16 Let us then approach God's throne of grace with confidence, so that we may receive mercy and find grace to help us in our time of need.

Did you get that? You approach, receive, find. The grace of God is so huge. It is so much bigger than our sin. God loves to lavish us with His grace; His kindness. We must never take it for granted and grieve the Holy Spirit by calling ourselves "Christians" and living any way we want to. If we can do that, God's seed is not in us and our salvation was not real. The blood sanctified you, set you apart from the world and made you holy. Salvation is life changing. That's why people use the term "converted." It means you switched from one side to the other. Salvation changes you inside and out. You belong to Jesus now. Being saved makes you want to obey God. The Holy Spirit that now lives in you makes you aware of your sin so you can deal with it.

1 Peter 1:23 For you have been born again, not of perishable seed, but of imperishable, through the living and enduring word of God.

1 John 3:8-10 The one who does what is sinful is of the devil, because the devil has been sinning from the beginning. The reason the Son of God appeared was to destroy the devil's work. No one who is born of God will continue to sin, because God's seed remains in them; they cannot go on sinning, because they have been born of God. This is how we know who the children of God are: Anyone who does not do what is right is not God's child, nor is anyone who does not love their brother and sister.

Hebrews 10:29 How much more severely do you think someone deserves to be punished who has trampled the Son of God underfoot, who has treated as an unholy thing the blood of the covenant that sanctified them, and who has insulted the Spirit of grace?

Achan abused the grace of God willingly for his own benefit. That's willful, presumptuous sin. As Christians, we have abused the Grace of God willingly for our own benefit by using the blood of Jesus as a license to sin freely. We sin freely because we don't have a relationship with Jesus. We can't hear the Holy Spirit in our hearts that convicts us of our sins. We have listened to the world and are taking our cues from strangers. We have stored the world in our hearts to get what we want and the prize is death. We don't know Jesus because we have not bothered to spend time with Him in His Word. God is finished with His work. Salvation is complete. Jesus has won. The Word of God tells us what we must do to be saved. It is not a salvation won by works. It is because you believed in what Jesus did on the cross. That is faith. That is what saved you. Then it tells us what to do after we are saved. That is where "works" or "deeds" come in and that is where the church falls short. What did you do with your faith after you got saved? Where is your fruit? We have been created in Christ Jesus (born again) to do good works after we are saved.

Ephesians 2:8-10 For it is by grace you have been saved, through faith – and this not from yourselves, it is the gift of God – not by works, so that no one can boast. For we are God's workmanship, created in Christ Jesus to do good works, which God prepared in advance for us to do.

2 Corinthians 13:5 Examine yourselves to see whether you are in the faith; test yourselves. Do you not realize that Christ Jesus is in you – unless, of course you fail the test?

The test is the love of God in your hearts and the way you live your life. When God was teaching the Israelites, He taught them as a corporate body. He spoke to them through the patriarchs, priests and prophets. Now, because of the blood of Jesus, God speaks to us individually.

Psalm 103:11-12 For as high as the heavens are above the earth, so great is his love for those who fear him; as far as the east is from the west, so far has he removed our transgressions from us.

We are His church. He lives in our hearts because we are His temple. He speaks to each of us in His Word through his Holy Spirit. Salvation is not where we end, it is where we begin. Grace gets us to salvation and beyond. Then mercy, justice, judgment, knowledge, discretion, wisdom, obedience, discipline and blessings follow. Welcome to the family of God! It is a life of promised abundance. We just have to choose it. We have a personal relationship with God through His Son Jesus and His Holy Spirit. We have the Holy Bible, the Word of God to encourage and train and warn us.

Psalm 119:89 Your word, O Lord, is eternal; it stands firm in the heavens.

Psalm 119:160 All your words are true; all your righteous laws are eternal.

Proverbs 30:5 Every word of God is flawless; he is a shield to those who take refuge in him.

2 Timothy 3:15-17 And how from infancy you have known the holy Scriptures, which are able to make you wise for salvation through faith in Christ Jesus. All Scripture is God-breathed and is useful for teaching, rebuking, correcting and training in righteousness, so that the man of God may be thoroughly equipped for every good work.

John 10:9-10 (NKJV) I am the door. If anyone enters by Me, he will be saved and will go in and out and find pasture. The thief does not come except to steal and kill and destroy. I have come that they may have life, and that they may have it more abundantly.

John 10:27-30 (NKJV) My sheep hear My voice, and I know them, and they follow Me. And I give them eternal life, and they shall never perish; neither shall anyone snatch them out of My hand. My Father, who has given them to Me, is greater than all; and no one is able to snatch them out of My Father's hand. I and My Father are one."

When we belong to Jesus, we are His sheep. Read this verse carefully because it describes the sheep that have eternal life. His sheep hear His voice because they have spent time with Him in His Word. His sheep follow Him because they are obedient to the Word. Jesus recognizes His obedient sheep and they will never perish. No one can snatch us out of the Fathers hands.

Read what God told John concerning the very end:

Revelations 21:5-8 He who was seated on the throne said, "I am making everything new!" Then he said, "Write this down, for these words are trustworthy and true." He said to me: "It is done. I am the Alpha and the Omega, the Beginning and the end. To him who is thirsty I will give to drink without cost from the spring of the water of life. He who overcomes will inherit all this, and I will be his God and he will be my son. But the cowardly, the unbelieving, the vile, the murderers, the sexually immoral, those who practice magic arts (drugs), the idolaters and all liars – their place will be in the fiery lake of burning sulfur. This is the second death."

This was so important for everyone to know that God told John to write it down because the words are trustworthy and true. Only he who overcomes receives the inheritance. You have to overcome your sin that you love.

Revelation 2:11 He who has an ear, let him hear what the Spirit says to the churches. He who overcomes will not be hurt at all by the second death.

Revelation 2:7 He who has an ear, let him hear what the Spirit says to the churches. To him who overcomes, I will give the right to eat from the tree of life, which is in the paradise of God.

Revelation 2:17b To him who overcomes, I will give some of the hidden manna.

Revelation 2:26 To him who overcomes and does my will to the end, I will give authority over the nations.

Revelation 3:11-13 I am coming soon. Hold on to what you have, so that no one will take your crown. Him who overcomes I will make a pillar in the temple of my God. Never again will he leave it. I will write on him the name of my God and the name of the city of my God, the new Jerusalem, which is coming down out of heaven from my God; and I will also write on him my new name.

Revelation 3:21 To him who overcomes, I will give the right to sit with me on my throne, just as I overcame and sat down with my Father on his throne.

Never think for one minute that you cannot lose your salvation by your deeds after you are saved. We have to overcome sin in our lives. Our lives will tell God and others about our faith. Our "deeds" do matter. The fallen angels and Satan and Adam and Eve all believed in God. It was their "deeds" that got them kicked out of the presence of God and it is our "deeds" and the way we live our lives that will determine our inheritance and prove our love for God after we are saved. Jesus says we cannot enter heaven with soiled robes. He knows our deeds.

Revelation 3:4-5 Yet you have a few people in Sardis who have not soiled their clothes. They will walk with me, dressed in white, for they are worthy. He who overcomes will, like them, be dressed in white. I will never blot out his name from my book of life, but will acknowledge his name before my Father and his angels.

Revelation 3:8 I know your deeds. See, I have placed before you an open door that no one can shut. I know that you have little strength, yet you have kept my word and have not denied my name.

Revelation 3:15-16 I know your deeds, that are neither cold nor hot. I wish you were either one or the other! So, because you are luke-warm – neither hot nor cold – I am about to spit you out of my mouth.

Revelation 3:19 Those whom I love I rebuke and discipline. So be earnest, and repent.

God watches our deeds after we are saved. Christians who are still sinning and have not repented before they die or by the time God comes back are not going to heaven. God will not recognize them. They did not bear fruit and their lives do not show that they have a relationship with God. Jesus talked about the importance of bearing good fruit.

John 15:5-8 "I am the vine; you are the branches. If you remain in me and I in you, you will bear much fruit; apart from me you can do nothing. If you do not remain in me, you are like a branch that is thrown away and withers; such branches are picked up, thrown into the fire and burned. If you remain in me and my words remain in you, ask whatever you wish, and it will be done for you. This is to my Father's glory, that you bear much fruit, showing yourselves to be my disciples.

Read those verses over and over again until you understand every word in every sentence. You have to show yourself to be God's disciple by your works or deeds after you get saved. It is impossible for us to be perfect, but our lives and the way we live after we ask Jesus into our hearts will change because of His Holy Spirit living in us.

Jesus is the vine. We have to stay attached to the vine to bear fruit. You have the choice to remain in Jesus and keep His words in you. If you get saved and willfully choose disobedience, you will wither and die. You cannot bear fruit that shows God you are His disciple when you are living in presumptuous sin. You didn't make the choice to get to know God and His Son Jesus by reading the Bible. You cannot be a disciple if you don't know whom you serve. The really terrible thing is that you will take others with

229

you. If you stay with the vine, (Jesus) and His words (the Bible) remain in you, you will bear much fruit and God will see that you are truly a disciple of His Son, Jesus. It glorifies God when we bear fruit. The fruit is the natural result of a life walked with God. It is what happens when God is our Father. It is salvation, miracles, direction, answered prayer, blessings, knowledge and understanding, discernment, love, joy, peace, patience, kindness, goodness, faithfulness, gentleness and self-control.

Isaiah 3:10 Tell the righteous it will be well with them, for they will enjoy the fruit of their deeds.

Jesus says we can ask whatever we wish and it will be done for us. When you are walking with God and obeying His Word, the things you wish for will line up with the will of God. God absolutely loves to bless His children. Bear fruit. Tell others about Jesus. Live a life of holiness.

Matthew 5:16 In the same way, let your light shine before men, that they may see your good deeds and praise your Father in heaven.

The tree of the knowledge of good and evil is never mentioned in the Bible again. Its work was finished. The choice had been made and yeast of that sin continues to spread today. But the tree of life is alive and well in the New Jerusalem. If you made the wrong choice, it is not too late. God's grace and the blood of Jesus are still available.

Revelation 22:1-2 Then the angel showed me the river of the water of life, as clear as crystal, flowing from the throne of God and of the Lamb down the middle of the great street of the city. On each side of the river stood the tree of life, bearing twelve crops of fruit, yielding its fruit every month. And the leaves of the tree are for the healing of the nations.

The Bible, the indisputable Word of God, is written for the redeemed. It is for the church of God. It is the unsaved Christians guide to sinful living so we don't have to be unsaved after all. It is so we are not deceived into thinking we are saved when we are not and that we can sin willfully because we believe and still go to heaven. It is so we are not deceived by the deceiver like Adam and Eve and the angels before them. It is the redeemed man's guide to joyful living. It is the loveliest book of love ever written, a love letter to the churches by the hand of God. If you are really saved, how can you not read it and how can you not obey? Glorify God with your life and bear fruit.

Isaiah 61:10 I delight greatly in the Lord; my soul rejoices in my God. For he has clothed me with garments of salvation and arrayed me in a robe of righteousness, as a bridegroom adorns his head like a priest, and as a bride adorns herself with her jewels.

Revelation 22:14 "Blessed are those who wash their robes, that they may have the right to the tree of life and may go through the gates into the city.

Oh wash your robe so you will have the right to the tree of life and you can go through the gates into the city. God is speaking to His church here! He is warning the redeemed. He even gives us a list of the sins that will not be allowed in the gates. It is not a "works" salvation where you earn your way to heaven by what you do. It is a "saved" lifestyle that shows God who you are in Him. It's not what you do for God but how you live for Him by doing His commandments. It's your behavior after you ask Jesus in your heart that tells Him if your confession was real or not. Did you choose Him or the world? Are you a "Christian" who is involved in sins that the Bible says will keep you out of heaven even though you are a believer?

Proverbs 14:2 He whose walk is upright fears the Lord, but he whose ways are devious despises him.

There is joy in obedience but evil doesn't want you to know that. Let go of your sin. Live saved; wash your robes and obey

God so He will recognize you as one of His own or you will go to hell.

Ephesians 5:8-10 For you were once darkness, but now you are light in the Lord. Live as children of light (for the fruit of the light consists in all goodness, righteousness and truth) and find out what pleases the Lord.

Revelation 21:7-8 He who overcomes will inherit all this, and I will be his God and he will be my son. But the cowardly, the unbelieving, the vile, the murderers, the sexually immoral, those who practice magic arts, the idolaters and all liars — their place will be in the fiery lake of burning sulfur. This is the second death."

Revelation 22:10-21 Then he told me, "Do not seal up the words of the prophecy of this scroll, because the time is near. Let the one who does wrong continue to do wrong; let the vile person continue to be vile; let the one who does right continue to do right; and let the holy person continue to be holy."

"Look, I am coming soon! My reward is with me, and I will give to everyone according to what he has done. I am the Alpha and the Omega, the First and the Last, the Beginning and the End. Blessed are those who wash their robes, that they may have the right to the tree of life and may go through the gates into the city. Outside are the dogs, those who practice magic arts, the sexually immoral, the murderers, the idolaters and everyone who loves and practices falsehood."

"I, Jesus, have sent my angel to give you this testimony for the churches. I am the Root and the Offspring of David, and the bright Morning Star."

The Sprit and the bride say, "Come!" And let the one who hears say, "Come!" Let the one who is thirsty come; and let the one who wishes take the free gift of the water of life.

I warn everyone who hears the words of the prophecy of this scroll: If anyone adds anything to them, God will add to that person the plagues described in this scroll.

And if anyone takes words away from this scroll of prophecy, God will take away from that person any share in the tree of life and in the Holy City, which are described in this scroll.

He who testifies to these things says, "Yes, I am coming soon."

Amen. Come, Lord Jesus

The grace of the Lord Jesus be with God's people.

Amen.

Chapter 10
THE ARMY AND THE FINAL DECISION

Psalm 119:18
Open my eyes that I may see wonderful things in your law.

W hen the Israelites were going through the desert, they followed God: The cloud by day and the pillar of fire by night. God spoke to the Israelites through Moses. The High Priest could be in God's presence only once a year when he went into the Most Holy Place to offer the atonement for sins. The relationship of the people with God was through Moses, the law that was read to them, the daily miracles they saw, the supernatural deliverance from their enemies, the tassels, the festivals, sacrifices, singing and the lifting of their hands in praise and worship.

There was not one day in all 40 years of their travels that they did not visually see the supernatural.

Exodus 40:38 So the cloud of the Lord was over the tabernacle by day, and fire was in the cloud by night, in the sight of all the house of Israel during all their travels.

They had a cloud that settled on the tabernacle in the day and this was not just any cloud. The bible says the cloud looked like fire (Numbers 9:15-23). It represented the Lord's presence among His people. There was no way you could mistake it for anything less than supernatural. There was a pillar of fire by night that was so bright a million people could see where they were going when they traveled after dark (Exodus 13:21-22, 40:36-38). They saw the waters part more than once so they could pass through on dry ground (Exodus 14:21-22, Joshua 3:13-17). They watched as God Himself lit the fire on the sacrifices (Leviticus 9:23-24), and they heard God speak to Moses on Mt. Sinai (Exodus 19:9-11). Breakfast, lunch and dinner were waiting for them every morning for 40 years (Exodus 16:35). They were right there when the ground opened up and swallowed the rebellious (Numbers 16:31-33), and they were there when the walls of Jericho fell with no help from man (Joshua 6:20). They saw God destroy their enemies with their own eyes. They ate no bread or wine and their clothes and shoes did not wear out during their 40 years of wandering in the desert (Deuteronomy 29:5-6).

How then is it possible that the Israelite men brought Moabite women and their idols into tents illuminated by Gods pillar of fire? How did they walk past the cloud over the tabernacle with idols under their coats? How did they dare gather a day's worth of manna in the morning and bring it into their tents and serve the enemy? How could they leave the camp protected by the one true God to go to Shittim and indulge in sexual immorality? How did it happen that they joined in on the sacrifices and worship of the idol Baal of Peor while the tassels were hitting their legs? And what was he thinking when Zimri brought the Midianite woman Cozbi to the Tent of Meeting covered by the cloud of God before the eyes of Moses and the whole assembly while the people were weeping because of the judgment of God over these very things?

How do you live in sin and attend church together and worship and thank Jesus for the cross? How do you take an unsaved partner to the altar and ask God to bless your marriage after He has told us not to be unequally yoked? How can you engage in homosexuality and say God doesn't mind anymore and teach others the same? How do you lie and use God's name in vain with the same mouth that you worship the King of Kings and Lord of Lords with? How can you cheat and steal and murder with the same hands you raise in adoration to God? How do you fill your body with drugs and alcohol and expect the Holy Spirit to live there too? How can your eyes and ears fill your heart and mind with the Word of God when they are also set on porn, demons, the occult, ungodly books, games, movies and music? And how can you read the Word of God and your horoscope at the same time? You can't have one foot in the world and one foot in heaven and expect to be saved in the end.

Psalm 73:27 Those who are far from you will perish; you destroy all who are unfaithful to you.

Revelation 3:15-16 I know your deeds, that you are neither cold nor hot. I wish you were one or the other! So, because you are lukewarm – neither hot nor cold – I am about to spit you out of my mouth.

James 4:8 Come near to God and He will come near to you. Wash your hands, you sinners, and purify your hearts, you double-minded.

It is as simple as a decision. That's all. You just have to decide who you are going to follow. You can be led for only so long before you have to make your own decision to follow Jesus or not. It's all or nothing. Part of you won't do. Part of you is not strong enough to conquer the enemy. You will completely fall. The story of the Israelites in the Old Testament is your story too. It was written for you so you, too, could see the miracles of God and the promise of Jesus and teach them to your children and your children's children.

God, Moses, the priests, kings, prophets and judges led the Israelites. Yet we read about very few Israelites that decided once and for all that their allegiance was to God alone forever. No more wavering, no more being tossed about by every wind of doctrine that comes along. No more putting God on a shelf and taking Him out when they needed Him. They all had the knowledge of God in common. There was no doubt that God was God because of everything they had seen and heard. It just came down to a choice: God's way or my way.

We can trace the decision pattern all the way back to Cain and Able. Cain, Ishmael, the daughters of Lot, Esau, Eli's sons Hophni and Phinehas, Saul, Absalom, kings and queens and princes etc., all who knew God but chose their own way instead and influenced entire nations to fall with them. The enemy may have had a hand in it, but the blame lies on the decision maker alone. Ultimately, you must decide for yourself who you will follow. Then you need to let God know that you accept the work of His Son on the cross and ask Jesus into your heart. After you do, your life needs to reflect your decision. The old things need to pass away and become new. It is not a works salvation. It is a lifestyle of obedience. Your life needs to reflect your decision to follow Christ. If it were not so, God would not have instructed Cain to master sin. If our lifestyle didn't matter, if sin was no longer an issue after the cross, if we are free to sin whenever we want because we believe in Jesus so we are saved anyway, God would not have told us to be holy because He is holy. Jesus would not have preached righteousness, holiness, obedience and repentance. What would be the point? How can you be saved and belong to the Creator when you live with the enemy?

If sin no longer matters and everyone is going to heaven anyway, then God is a liar and a hypocrite. The flood was a waste of time. The death of Jesus was unnecessary and the cross a lie. All who died in the forty years of wandering in the desert died for nothing. All the nations God disposed of for their evil was for nothing. Forgiveness is a sham. God's wrath is not to be feared and the Word of God, our Bible, has no power and is dead. Wouldn't Satan be thrilled if he could get God's people to believe that? If we believe the lie that our sins don't matter, Satan will win our company in hell. It is easy to know when something is from the enemy because it is always the opposite of what God tells us in His Word. But how can you possibly know what that is if you don't spend time with God by reading the Bible?

God led us all the way to the cross. Then it was done. Our sins are forgiven forever. The law is complete. We can enter into God's presence ourselves without going through the priests and we have the Holy Spirit, one called alongside to help, to be our guide. Everything is finished perfectly. We are left with only one thing: a decision. And if that decision is to follow God through His Son Jesus Christ with the help of the Holy Spirit, the next step is to master sin. It is so easy and yet the enemy wants to make it so hard. You just die to yourself. Do what God wants you to do, not what you want to do. You follow Jesus' example. Do what He said. Jesus said He came to give us abundant life. You will not regret your decision. Jesus is good! You will have the help of the Holy Spirit and the Word of God, the Bible, to help you when you need it. You will need it! You also have prayer. The single most powerful weapon in your arsenal is prayer.

Psalm 66:16-20 Come and hear, all you who fear God; let me tell you what he has done for me. I cried out to him with my mouth; his praise was on my tongue. If I had cherished sin in my heart, the Lord would not have listened; but God has surely listened and has heard my prayer. Praise be to God, who has not rejected my prayer or withheld his love from me!

How you live your life matters very much to God. You must lay aside your way for God's way. The enemy wants you to think it's hard. He wants you to think you will be miserable and sad and that God doesn't love you because He won't let you behave that way. The truth is, it is a little, tiny fence line decision that takes seconds to speak out. Quit thinking about what you will be missing and bring all your thoughts captive into the obedience of Christ.

239

2 Corinthians 10:5 We demolish arguments and every pretension that sets itself up against the knowledge of God, and we take captive every thought to make it obedient to Christ.

There is no argument or pretention that can win against what God has told us. It is either yes or no. Your fence line conversation with God should go like this:

Lord, I don't understand why I can't do this, but I read in your Word that you said "no" so I am not going to do _____ anymore because I love you more than what I am giving up. I am more concerned about obeying you; following your will and loving you back than I am about getting my own way. I know you will fill me with your joy and your Holy Spirit will comfort me and understanding will follow my commitment to you. I lay aside my desires for yours. Beginning this second, I am not listening to the enemy or the world. I will follow you and obey your Word for the rest of my days and the joy of the Lord will be my strength. Amen.

Don't let the enemy put contradictory thoughts in your mind about your new decision. Start acting on your decision immediately. If you don't act on your decision right away, the enemy will try to change your mind. Find a Christian who is obedient in these areas to be with you and help you. If you are a woman, find a woman to help. If you are a man, find a man to help. Obedience feels good. It is a relief to follow God.

God's grace, His unmerited favor is at work in all of us who love Him. Like David, when we repent of our sins, we are always forgiven. The key is repentance, turning away from your sins. When David sinned and then repented for it, he never did it again. He intentionally obeyed God and led Israel to do the same.

Hebrews 4:12-13 For the word of God is living and active. Sharper than any double-edged sword, it penetrates even to dividing soul and spirit, joints and marrow; it judges the thoughts and attitudes of the heart. *Nothing in all creation is hidden from God's sight. Everything is uncovered and laid bare before the eyes of him to whom we must give account.*

If what we do is not important to God, why then does His Word judge the thoughts and attitudes of the heart? Why do we have to give an account to God for everything we have done if what we do is not important? Why does He command us to be holy and walk in all His ways?

Philippians 4:4-8 Rejoice in the Lord always. I will say it again: Rejoice! Let your gentleness be evident to all. The Lord is near. Do not be anxious about anything, but in everything, by prayer and petition, with thanksgiving, present your requests to God. And the peace of God, which transcends all understanding, will guard your hearts and your minds in Christ Jesus. Finally, brothers, whatever is true, whatever is noble, whatever is right, whatever is pure, whatever is lovely, whatever is admirable-if anything is excellent or praiseworthy-think about such things.

You may not understand why God says some of the things He does and why He requires us to be obedient. You might not understand why He tells you to do or not do something, but out of faith and obedience to the Lord your God, you just do it. Your faith will express itself in your obedience. His faithfulness will see you through and joy and everlasting life will be your reward.

Psalm 128:1-6 Blessed are all who fear the Lord, who walk in his ways. You will eat the fruit of your labor; blessings and prosperity will be yours. Your wife will be like a fruitful vine within your house; your sons will be like olive shoots around your table. Thus is the man blessed who fears the Lord. May the Lord bless you from Zion all the days of your life; may you see the prosperity of Jerusalem, and may you live to see your children's children. Peace be upon Israel.

Amen and Amen.

78914410R00137

Made in the USA
Columbia, SC
22 October 2017